Don't Panic—
Dinner's
in the Freezer

Don't Panic— Dinner's in the Freezer

Great-Tasting Meals You Can Make Ahead

Susie Martinez
Vanda Howell
Bonnie Garcia

Revell

Grand Rapids, Michigan

Published by Fleming H. Revell
a division of Baker Publishing Group
P.O. Box 6287, Grand Rapids, MI 49516-6287
www.revellbooks.com

Third printing, September 2006

Printed in the United States of America

The Library of Congress-in-Publication Data
Martinez, Susie.
    Don't panic, dinner's in the freezer : great-tasting meals you can make ahead / Susie Martinez, Vanda Howell, Bonnie Garcia.
        p. cm.
    Includes bibliographical references and index.
    ISBN 10: 0-8007-3055-0 (pbk.)
    ISBN 978-0-8007-3055-0 (pbk.)
    1. Make-ahead cookery. 2. Quick and easy cookery. 3. Cookery (Frozen foods) I. Howell, Vanda. II. Garcia, Bonnie. III. Title.
    TX652.M2935 2005
    641.5'55—dc22   2005014325

The recipe for the Pinwheel Flank Steak pictured on the front cover is found on page 143.

We lovingly dedicate this book to our most excellent and awesome husbands, Joe, Steve, and Mike, for supporting and encouraging us throughout the Don't Panic journey.

To our children, Chris, Cassie, Nathan, Daniel, Jonathan, and Elliott. We love you!

Contents

Preface   9

Acknowledgments   10

Introduction   11

The Don't Panic Method of Cooking   12

    Let's Go Shopping!   15

    Now We're Cookin'   17

    Cooking Day Suggestions   19

    Packaging and Freezing the Goods   21

    How Long Will It Keep?   25

    Keeping Others in Mind   27

Appetizers and Beverages   29

Breads and Muffins   45

Soup's On   61

Poultry   79

Beef and Pork   117

Pasta and More   159

Now for Dessert   177

Brunch Items   203

Add a Side Dish   221

Equivalency Chart   233

Bibliography   234

Index of Recipes   235

Preface

The "Don't Panic" method of cooking began in 1990 when one new mother (Susie Martinez) quit her job and was home alone all day with a colicky baby and a reduced household income. At that time, it was not a developed method of cooking to be shared with others. It was a means of survival that helped her through a tough time.

In short, instead of cooking dinner each evening, she cooked one recipe once a week in large quantity. One meal was eaten for dinner that evening, and three more were frozen for another time. With a variety of meals in her freezer, dinner became a pleasant oasis instead of one more headache at the end of a long, hard day.

A lot has happened since 1990. This new mother began cooking with two of her friends, and they began to share what they were doing with others. The system is now called the Don't Panic method of cooking, a fun new cookbook has been published, and presentations are being given across the country. But over time the idea has remained the same, because the need never changes. We encourage you to read on and learn how easy it is to simplify your life through the Don't Panic method of cooking!

Acknowledgments

We offer thanks to God for the opportunity to publish this book and for blessing our lives so abundantly. Without his provision, this book would not be possible.

Countless thanks to our moms, Colleen, Shirley, and Flo, for instilling in us an appreciation for good home-cooked meals and the value of family mealtime. We hope to pass this legacy on to our children.

Thanks to our dear friend Jeanie Wilking, who has been our prayer warrior through the ups and downs of our endeavors.

Special thanks to Marita Littauer for giving us encouragement and a vision for the publication of this book.

Introduction

It's three o'clock in the afternoon . . . do you know what you're having for dinner tonight? If that question sends a wave of panic through your already-harried mind, then this cookbook is for you!

For most of us, the June Cleaver era has ended. No longer do we have time to stay at home all day, keeping our houses spotless and preparing wonderful meals. As a result of the new, hectic lifestyles we face, people are hiring more household help and eating an increasing number of take-out items, fast food, and prefrozen meals.

But take heart! We have developed an easy, economical, and enjoyable alternative to traditional meal preparation. After speaking to hundreds of women and receiving feedback from many of the people presently using our cookbook, we can assure you that this book will help you—whoever you are!

The Don't Panic method of cooking is being used by

- Hungry professionals
- Working parents
- Stay-at-home moms (or dads!)
- Retired, elderly, or widowed people
- People who eat (this means you!)

Once you try this method, you will have a hard time returning to the way you used to cook. So grab this book, grab a friend, and embark on a whole new cooking experience! Then next Tuesday at five o'clock, when you're peering into your refrigerator and there's nothing for dinner . . . *Don't Panic—Dinner's in the Freezer!*

The Don't Panic Method of Cooking

This book is your guide for preparing healthy, gourmet-style meals available at a moment's notice. We hope it becomes an invaluable tool in your cooking. Its design lets you prepare numerous meals with minimal effort, which means you will spend less time, money, and energy cooking better meals than ever. The recipes in this book have been freezer-tested and refined.

Here are five practical steps that will be helpful in making the Don't Panic method of cooking easy to implement.

Step One: Get Started

The Don't Panic cooking method can be implemented simply by choosing your favorite family recipe and doubling or tripling it. For example, if you are making Cranberry Chicken, triple the recipe, have one for dinner that evening, and then put the other two meals in the freezer to serve at a later time. In its simplest form, making recipes in quantity is what the Don't Panic method is all about.

Step Two: Choose a Day

Preplanned activities that actually make it to the calendar tend to be the ones that get done. Practically speaking, this step requires looking at your daily and weekly responsibilities and choosing a block of time out of that week for cooking. This may involve a weekday morning or afternoon if you are home during the day; it may be an evening or on the weekend if you work full-time outside the home.

Step Three: Check Weekly Loss Leaders

The term *loss leaders* refers to items that supermarkets sell below cost and at a loss to entice you to shop at their store. The other items you buy while shopping make up for the loss the store takes on loss leaders.

Supermarkets usually rotate their loss leaders on a weekly basis. Stores will promote these items through weekly advertisements distributed in a local newspaper or through the mail. To track loss leaders, you will need to consistently consult weekly supermarket ads. You will soon know when these ads are distributed and how long a supermarket sale is effective. As you do this regularly, it becomes easier to recognize and take advantage of great loss leaders.

To illustrate how you can save big by buying loss leaders, consider this example, which uses Chicken Enchiladas as the Don't Panic entrée. If you are cooking with two friends, you will need approximately fifteen pounds of boneless chicken. If boneless chicken is a loss leader in a local supermarket, it will be advertised at around $1.99 per pound. That's $29.85 for fifteen pounds of chicken. On the other hand, if the chicken was purchased at the regular price of $3.99 per pound, you would have spent $59.85. By simply shopping loss leaders and planning your cooking menu accordingly, you just saved $30.00 on the meat item alone! By doing this consistently, you will never pay full price for your entrées.

Another important way to make the Don't Panic cooking method economically beneficial is to custom package according to what your family will actually eat rather than according to the directions in the recipe. Custom packaging is described in detail in the "Packaging and Freezing the Goods" chapter on page 21. By simply shopping loss leaders and custom packaging by family size, your savings can be incredible! Each entrée included in this book should average between $3.50 and $4.25 to feed a family of four. Please note that this cost is per family, not per person.

Step Four: Choose Your Recipes for Cooking Day

After checking local ads to determine weekly loss leaders, choose one or two recipes for cooking day that use those discounted items. For example, if beef is on sale, choose beef entrées for cooking day (Teriyaki Steak and Beef Stroganoff, for example). The key is to avoid paying full price for meat items. Cook according to what is on sale!

Occasionally there will be a week when you can't use a loss leader to cook entrées. During those weeks, you can still avoid paying full price for meat items by having a baking day instead. Choose from muffins, rolls, breads, pizza dough, cookies, or desserts. These items freeze very well if you follow appropriate packaging instructions. See "Packaging and Freezing the Goods" on page 21.

Step Five: Construct Your Shopping List

Your shopping list should be made before going to the grocery store. By using the quantity tables found in this book, you can accurately determine the amount of each ingredient you will need for each recipe. For example, if you are cooking by yourself and tripling the recipe, refer to the "x3" column for correct quantities. If you are cooking with two other people and are each tripling the recipe, refer to the "x9" column. For more grocery-shopping tips, see the next chapter, "Let's Go Shopping!"

Let's Go Shopping!

Over the years as we have cooked together, we have come across some shopping tips that will be very helpful as you begin the Don't Panic cooking method.

One: The Value of Warehouse Stores

As we speak to many groups, one of the most frequently asked questions is "What about shopping at warehouse stores?" We have found that warehouse stores (Sam's Club and Costco, for example) are great for certain large-quantity items, like cooking oil, flour, sugar, nuts, and cheese; and freezing supplies, like freezer bags, disposable gloves, wider-width aluminum foil, and plastic wrap. For these items, you can save more by shopping at warehouse stores instead of grocery stores, even if you're using coupons!

For example, we purchased the wider-width plastic wrap (which contains two thousand square feet) at a warehouse store for approximately eight or nine dollars. Two years later, and after a lot of use, we're still using the same roll.

If the cost of an annual membership is a concern, consider sharing a membership with your cooking partners. One person can buy the membership, and you can split the cost among you. Warehouse stores usually allow a member to bring in guests when shopping.

One note: we have found that supermarket sales offer greater savings on most meats if you shop the loss leaders.

Two: Invest in a Community Box

If you regularly cook with other people, you might consider investing in a community box. You can use this box to store bulk-quantity items that are regularly used on cooking day. The items you keep in your community box might include freezer bags, foil, plastic wrap, vegetable oil, spices, flour, sugar, and salt. Buy these items in large quantity and divide the cost among the members of your cooking team. Although you may pay more for them initially, in the long run, your savings will be great!

Three: Get to Know Your Butcher

When you need large quantities of meat cut, you can save time by asking your supermarket butcher to cut it for you. For example, if you're making Beef Stroganoff, you can ask your butcher to cut your sirloin "fajita" style. Or if you're making Shish-Ka-Bobs, you can ask your butcher to cube the beef. If your recipe calls for flattened chicken breasts, have your butcher run the chicken breasts through a meat tenderizer machine.

Having your meat cut ahead of time will save you hours on cooking day! Most stores offer this service as a courtesy at no extra charge. Just be sure to give your butcher some extra time. Call ahead and place your order, or have your butcher do it while you shop.

Four: Shop the Day before Cooking

It's best to do your shopping the day before your cooking day. This will allow you to get an early start on cooking day. If cooking with friends, it usually works to have one person shop for the whole group. On cooking day, bring your receipts, divide the costs, and reimburse the shopper.

Now you're ready to start cooking!

Now We're Cookin'

Here are some helpful hints for cooking day.

One: Organize Your Groceries

On cooking day, assemble all groceries and ingredients necessary for the recipes you'll be preparing. If you are cooking with others, check the community box (see "Invest in a Community Box" on page 15) for any of the bulk items needed for cooking or packaging.

Two: Prepare Your Ingredients

Read through your recipes to determine what items need to be prepared. If you're cooking with others, divide up and assign each person a task. To make cleanup easier, keep a sink full of soapy water available. When you're finished with a pan or utensil, let it soak while you're completing the recipe.

- Chop all the vegetables first. If you're preparing two different entrées on cooking day, refer to both recipes to see what steps can be combined in food preparation. For example, if both of the dishes call for chopped onions, chop all of the onions you need for both. Then set aside the appropriate quantity of onions for each recipe.
- Prepare the meat or poultry. If the meat or poultry item you're using needs to be cut up or browned, do that next. You may want to have your butcher cut your meat for you. See "Get to Know Your Butcher" on page 16.
- Measure out any liquid or dry ingredients needed. To save time and effort, refer to the equivalency chart in the back of this book when measuring large quantities of ingredients. For example, if you need twelve teaspoons of an ingredient when doubling or tripling a recipe, refer to the chart and measure out four tablespoons or one-fourth cup instead.

Three: Follow the Recipe as Written

Begin to assemble all the prepared ingredients according to the recipe's directions. If you're doubling or tripling a recipe, be prepared by having two or three separate mixing bowls or pans to accommodate the larger quantities of food ingredients. Also see "Custom Cooking" on page 19.

Four: Cool Food

When applicable, let the prepared food cool and come to room temperature. Doing so will help prevent the ice crystals that form when hot or warm food is packaged prematurely. To speed the cooling process, place pot holders on the shelves in your refrigerator, then place the warm food on the pot holders. Be sure that the hot pans do not touch anything else in your refrigerator. When cool, package according to your family size. See "Packaging and Freezing the Goods" on page 21.

Cooking Day Suggestions

One: Finishing Up

We use the "cool down" time to clean up, eat lunch, feed the kids, and calculate our grocery receipts to reimburse the shopper. Then we custom package our meals and go home with a lot of great meals and a wonderful feeling of accomplishment and success.

Two: Trying New Recipes

On your cooking day, in addition to the meals you plan to prepare and freeze, try one new recipe for dinner that night (using the same loss leader you're cooking with that day). If it's a keeper, add it to your repertoire of recipes. You also might consider preparing a very small portion to see how it freezes. Be sure to make notes to yourself so you can change, correct, or customize the recipe according to your family's likes and dislikes.

Three: Custom Cooking

"I couldn't sneak a chopped onion or green pepper past my family no matter how deeply I buried them in the dish!" Don't let picky tastes or food allergies discourage you. Custom cooking lets you adapt your meals according to your family's likes and dislikes by simply adding or omitting ingredients in a particular recipe.

If cooking with a friend, you can accommodate family preferences by designating a separate pan on the stove for each family. This allows you to customize the recipe according to your family's tastes and needs.

Four: Keeping Baked Goods Moist

- Muffins: When baking, you might consider slightly underbaking muffins until almost done but not doughy. Muffins should be only slightly browned on top. This will ensure a moist, fresh-baked taste when reheating.

- Breads and quick breads: These should be completely baked. Be careful not to overbake so that moisture is not lost.
- Quiches: Bake quiches just until a knife inserted in the center comes out clean. This keeps the quiche from drying out when reheating on serving day.

Packaging and Freezing the Goods

As you consider using the Don't Panic method of cooking, one obstacle you may face is the lack of a separate freezer in which to store large quantities of food. We encourage you to begin working with the space that you do have available. By incorporating some of the hints we offer regarding custom packaging and freezing, you will be able to store quite a few meals in your refrigerator's freezer alone. As our cooking method becomes more a part of your lifestyle, you may want to make an investment in a chest or upright freezer. This will allow you to prepare larger quantities of meals, as well as take better advantage of sale items at your local grocery store.

One: Custom Packaging

An essential component of the economic savings of the Don't Panic method is to package meals according to your family size. On cooking day, after you have prepared your recipes and you are ready to put them into the freezer, package your meals according to how much your family will eat at each meal.

For example, if preparing a recipe of Chicken Enchiladas with a yield of eight enchiladas per recipe, tripling the recipe will provide three casserole dishes of eight enchiladas each. This is a total of twenty-four enchiladas. If your family eats only six enchiladas for dinner, the enchiladas can be repackaged into meals containing six enchiladas each. You have now made four meals instead of three! This stretches your loss leader savings even more.

Two: A Word about Containers

In choosing containers to freeze our meals in, we have found that high-quality freezer bags (not storage bags) work well in most cases. As a general rule, plastic containers take up too much space in your freezer and should be passed up for more space-saving techniques.

Three: Flash Freezing

Some meals can go directly into freezer bags or containers without any further shaping or extra wrapping. If a particular meal needs to hold its form, you may flash freeze it. This refers to putting an item in the freezer for a short period of time in order to freeze it into a particular shape. Once the food item is solid, it is removed from the "molding" or shaping container and placed in a freezer bag for storage.

Four: Methods of Freezing

A. Freezer Bag Method
- When to use it:
  - Liquid: Use this method when freezing items such as soup, chili, and stews.
  - Semi-solid food items: Use this method when freezing items that DO NOT need to hold a particular form, such as meats in marinade, stroganoff, and barbecue shredded beef.
- How to do it: When using the freezer bag method for freezing, place your meal in the freezer bag, remove as much air as possible, and seal. Then take a cake pan, or a pan that has sides, and lay the bags flat, stacking one on top of the other. The cake pan will not only freeze the meals flat, giving you more freezer room, but will help ensure that any leaks will be kept within the pan. Place the pan in the freezer. Once the item has been "flash frozen" (see "Flash Freezing" above), remove the items from the pan and stack them inside your freezer.
- On serving day: When defrosting, make sure you place the item in the refrigerator with a pan, plate, or bowl underneath to catch the extra moisture (or any leaks) from defrosting. For your health and safe food handling, we do not recommend defrosting the meal on the kitchen countertop, as this promotes the growth of harmful bacteria. If you need to speed up the defrosting process, consider using the defrost cycle on your microwave oven.

B. Foil and Plastic Wrap Method
- When to use it:
  - Semi-solid food items: Use this method when freezing items that DO need to hold a particular form, such as Chicken Enchiladas, Cottage Pie, lasagna, and meatloaf.

- How to do it: When using the foil and plastic wrap method for freezing, line your baking dish with aluminum foil first and then with a layer of plastic wrap (make sure that the foil and plastic wrap are large enough to cover the bottom, sides, and top of the dish). If your food is hot, allow it to cool slightly. Fill the dish with your prepared meal. When completely cooled, seal the plastic wrap, removing as much air as possible. Then seal the outer aluminum foil layer. With the packaged meal still in the pan, place it in the freezer. Once the item has been flash frozen, slip the meal out of the pan and into a freezer bag. See "Flash Freezing" on page 22.
- On serving day: Remove the meal from the freezer and thaw slightly. Remove foil and plastic wrap, then place in original dish for baking. If you have a little trouble getting the plastic wrap off, place the meal in the microwave or dip it in warm water quickly. The plastic wrap should then come off easily.
- Advantages of foil and plastic wrap method:
  - Baking dishes aren't tied up in the freezer.
  - The pans are removed after the meals are frozen solid, and then the meals will stack compactly in the freezer.
  - Your meal fits back into the original pan for thawing and baking or cooking.

C. Baked Goods
- To help ensure freshness and taste, always double wrap baked items. Wrap the item first with plastic wrap, then place in a freezer bag.
- Cookies: Cookie dough may be flash frozen by placing formed cookie balls on cookie sheets in the freezer for ten to twenty minutes. Remove and place in freezer bags. For slice-and-bake cookies, form cookie dough into "logs" (two to two and one-half inches in diameter). Wrap thoroughly with plastic wrap and seal ends well. Place logs in a freezer bag. Frozen cookie dough may go directly from freezer to the cookie sheet and be baked. Cookies may also be frozen after baking.
- On serving day: Baked breads and muffins can be brought to room temperature or defrosted in the microwave.

Five: Finishing Up

Date and label your meals (no one likes mystery meals!). Also note specific cooking time and temperature and any special recipe instructions. Label meals directly on the freezer bag using a permanent marker. Freezer moisture will sometimes cause tape labels to fall off.

Six: Miscellaneous Freezing Hints

- Reuse your freezer bags when possible. Freezer bags used to store uncooked chicken, beef, or pork or marinated meals should not be reused. Bags that were used for baked goods or as the outer, second-layer wrap can be used many times.
- Freeze leftover tomato paste in one-tablespoon portions. A lot of recipes call for only that amount. Wrap each tablespoon portion in plastic wrap, then place it inside a small freezer bag. When you need tomato paste, it's available!
- Wrap leftover fresh cilantro in plastic wrap and put it in a small freezer bag. When needed, add it directly to your recipe.
- After squeezing the juice from lemons, oranges, and limes, store and freeze the leftover halved rinds in freezer bags. When a recipe calls for fresh peel (for example, Chocolate-Orange Crumb Cake or Orange Sour Cream Loaf), simply grate the frozen rind. You get a fresh citrus taste without having to keep fruit on hand.
- Fresh ginger grates easily when frozen and keeps a long time. Wrap it in plastic wrap and place in a freezer bag.
- Season and slow-cook roasts (when they are on sale as a loss leader) and shred. Freeze one- to two-cup portions in freezer bags for quick soft tacos or burritos.

How Long Will It Keep?

Your goal should be to have a constant rotation of meals going into and coming out of your freezer. However, there will be times when a meal is in the freezer for a number of months and you question whether or not it is still good or safe to eat.

By following the packaging directions given in this book, you will maximize the length of time your meals will taste fresh and remain free from freezer burn. In general, after meals have been in your freezer for more than three to six months, they begin to lose premium texture and flavor. Although these meals do not pose a health risk when eaten, they may not have the optimal quality they had when you first prepared them.

The following chart provides general guidelines for optimal freezing times.

Meals		
Cooked meat and poultry in sauces (e.g., Chicken Pot Pies, Beef Stroganoff)		5–6 months
Uncooked meat and poultry in sauces or marinades (e.g., Cranberry Chicken, Teriyaki Steak)		see Raw Meats
Spaghetti sauce, chili, soups, stews		5–6 months
Quiche		3 months
Raw Meats		
Roasts	beef	7–9 months
	pork	4–6 months
Steaks	beef	7–9 months
	pork	2–3 months
Pork chops, ribs		2–3 months
Ground beef		3 months
Chicken		10 months
Turkey	whole	6 months
	parts	4–6 months

Baked Goods

Quick breads	2–3 months
Muffins	3 months
Yeast breads or rolls	2–3 months
Pizza dough	5–6 months
Cookies	3–4 months
Frozen desserts	1–3 months

Keeping Others in Mind

Using the Don't Panic method provides you with a creative way to help others by supplying them with a meal during stressful times. You will find that you always have a variety of meals available to pull out of your freezer and give to someone in need. Here are some examples of people who would appreciate your help.

- New moms: When a woman has a baby, whether it is her first or her last, she needs meals. Share a meal with a new mom, and watch her glow with appreciation!
- Singles: Most singles work all day and find it very difficult to come home and prepare a nutritious meal for one person. If you have a small amount of food left after packaging your meals on cooking day, make a portion for a single person that you know. It could be their first home-cooked meal in weeks!
- Bad day syndrome: Did your friend crash her car? Drop the eggs in the grocery store parking lot? Change her potty-training child's clothes five times by ten o'clock in the morning? Turn someone's terrible day into one with a bit more sunshine by supplying them with a meal for that evening.
- The elderly: Are you worried about your aging parents' eating habits? How about the elderly couple next door? It's very difficult for the elderly to keep up with meal preparation, and therefore we see them eating fewer meals with lower nutritional value. An excellent thing to do with the little bit of extra food you find at the end of your cooking day is to share it with an elderly parent or neighbor.
- Sickness or death: A whole family is thrown into turmoil when they encounter sickness or a death in the family. Bringing a meal is a tangible way to assist those you might otherwise feel powerless to help. Consider providing it in frozen form to be used when other help has faded away.

- Community freezer: If you belong to a church or civic organization, you might consider using the freezer in their kitchen to store meals to be taken to those in need. We have seen this be a wonderful tool for outreach within these organizations.

We all have friends, neighbors, and relatives who need our help on certain occasions. Although we have a genuine desire to help them, with today's busy schedules, it may be difficult to do so. The beauty of using the Don't Panic method of cooking is that it takes very little time, money, or energy to help those we care about in a substantial way. You can provide relief with a personal touch that will let them know you care.

Appetizers and Beverages

Apricot-Glazed Chicken Tenders
Apricot Nectar Slush
Caribbean Cooler
Elegant Mushroom Cups
Gourmet Palmiers
Holiday Fruit Punch
Kansas City Hot Wings
Orange Beef Lettuce Wraps
Refreshing Fruit Smoothies
Santa Fe Hot Dip
South of the Border Queso
Strawberry Freeze

Apricot-Glazed Chicken Tenders

Also great for a main dish

	x2	x4	x6
2 lbs. chicken tenders, cut-up breast pieces, or chicken wings, tips removed	4 lbs	8 lbs	12 lbs
Marinade			
⅓ cup vegetable oil	⅔c	1⅓c	2c
3 cloves garlic, minced	6	12	18
2 T. lemon juice	¼c	7T	½c + 2T
1 t. rosemary	2t	4t	2T
1 t. thyme	2t	4t	2T
salt and pepper, to taste (approx. ¼ t.)	½t	1t	1½t
1 small bay leaf, crumbled	2	4	6
Apricot glaze			
1 onion, minced	2	4	6
1 T. unsalted butter	2T	4T	6T
2 T. cider vinegar	¼c	½c	¾c
1 cup apricot preserves	2c	4c	6c
1 T. soy sauce	2T	¼c	6T
2 t. Dijon mustard	4t	2T + 2t	¼c
¼ t. ginger	½t	1t	1½t
¼ t. cloves	½t	1t	1½t
¼ t. salt	½t	1t	1½t
⅛ t. pepper	¼t	½t	¾t

Original recipe yields

4–6 servings

Cooking day instructions

For marinade: In large freezer bag, combine marinade ingredients. Add chicken pieces, toss to coat, and marinate at room temperature one hour. (If preparing for that day, chill 6–8 hours or overnight. Prepare glaze below and refrigerate.)

Meanwhile, prepare the apricot glaze following the directions below. After one hour of marinating time, freeze.

For apricot glaze: In saucepan, cook onion in butter over moderate heat, stirring until softened. Add vinegar and continue cooking until liquid has reduced by one-half. Add preserves, soy sauce, Dijon mustard, spices, salt, and pepper. Cook uncovered, stirring occasionally, for 10 minutes or until thick. Place mixture in a food processor or blender and puree. Freeze apricot glaze in a separate, smaller freezer bag. Store in freezer together with marinated chicken.

Serving day instructions

Thaw chicken pieces and discard marinade. Place chicken on rack of broiler pan and broil 6 inches from heat, 5 minutes on each side. Baste chicken generously with apricot glaze and broil 3 minutes on each side or until well glazed and brown. Adjust cooking time if using thicker cuts of chicken.

Hint

Chicken can also be prepared on a charcoal or gas grill. To bake chicken, place pieces in a large baking dish. Bake at 425 degrees for approximately 25–30 minutes, basting with apricot glaze and turning every 10 minutes. Do not overcook. Shortly before chicken is done, put the chicken under the broiler and broil until golden brown and bubbly.

Apricot Nectar Slush

Great for entertaining and special occasions!

	x2	x4	x6
4 tea bags	8	16	24
2 cups boiling water	4c	8c	12c
2 cups sugar	4c	8c	12c
5 cups cold water	10c	20c	30c
1-12 oz. can frozen lemonade concentrate	2	4	6
1-12 oz. can frozen orange juice concentrate	2	4	6
3 cups apricot nectar	6c	12c	18c

Serving day

Chilled club soda

Original recipe yields

15–20 servings

Cooking day instructions

Steep tea in boiling water in large bowl for 20 minutes. Add sugar, stirring until dissolved. Stir in cold water and cool. Stir in juices and nectar. Freeze mixture in a hard-sided container with lid. This makes it easier to scoop out and serve into glasses using an ice cream scoop.

Serving day instructions

Keep frozen until ready to serve. Fill serving glass ½ full with frozen mixture. Add club soda and stir until slushy.

Hint

Mixture freezes better if placed in several smaller containers.

Caribbean Cooler

Wonderful for brunch or entertaining

	x2
7 cups water	14c
2 cups sugar	4c
4 regular-size tea bags	8
1-12 oz. can frozen lemonade	2
1-6 oz. can limeade	2
1-12 oz. can frozen pineapple-orange-banana juice	2
2 cups pineapple juice	4c

Serving day

Chilled club soda

Mint leaves and lime slices, for garnish

Original recipe yields

10–12 servings

Cooking day instructions

In a large pan, combine water and sugar. Bring to a boil. Remove from heat and add the tea bags. Cover and let steep for 10 minutes. Cool. Remove tea bags and add lemonade, limeade, and juices. Stir together.

Freeze mixture in a hard-sided container with lid. This makes it easier to scoop out and serve into glasses using an ice cream scoop. Freeze at least 12 hours.

Serving day instructions

Fill serving glass ⅓ to ½ full with frozen mixture. Add club soda and stir. Garnish with mint leaves and lime slices and serve.

Hint

Mixture freezes better if placed in several smaller containers.

Elegant Mushroom Cups

Amazingly delicious!

	x2	x4
48 very thin slices of bread	96	192
4 T. margarine, room temperature	½c	1c
4 T. butter	½c	1c
3 T. green onions, finely chopped	6T	¾c
½ lb. mushrooms, very finely chopped	1 lb	2 lbs
2 T. flour	¼c	½c
1 cup heavy cream	2c	4c
1 T. minced fresh parsley	2T	4T
1½ t. minced chives	1T	2T
½ t. fresh lemon juice	1t	2t
½ t. salt	1t	2t
⅛ t. cayenne pepper	¼t	½t

Original recipe yields

48 mushroom cups

Cooking day instructions

Using a 2½-inch cookie cutter, cut a circle from each slice of bread. Lightly spread softened margarine on both sides of circles, and press into mini muffin tins to form cups. Bake 10 minutes at 350 degrees or until bread is lightly toasted. Set aside.

In a 10-inch skillet, melt butter. Add green onions and cook over moderate heat for 4 minutes, stirring constantly. Add mushrooms and cook for 10–15 minutes. Remove from heat and sprinkle flour over mixture, stirring to blend. Return to heat. Pour in heavy cream; stir and heat to boiling. When thickened, simmer and cook 1 minute. Remove from heat. Add parsley, chives, lemon juice, salt, and cayenne pepper. Cool.

Freeze cups and mushroom mixture separately, using freezer bag method.

Serving day instructions

Thaw mushroom mixture and cups. Preheat oven to 350 degrees. Fill cups just before baking. Bake 10 minutes. Let cool 5 minutes before serving.

Gourmet Palmiers

A unique blend of mushrooms and pastry

	x2	x4	x6
1 lb. fresh mushrooms	2 lbs	4 lbs	6 lbs
1½ medium onions, peeled and quartered	3	6	9
5 T. butter	10T	1¼c	1¾c + 2T
2 T. flour	¼c	½c	¾c
1 t. fresh lemon juice	2t	4t	2T
1 t. dried thyme	2t	4t	2T
½ t. Tabasco sauce	1t	2t	1T
Salt and pepper, to taste			
¼ cup heavy cream	½c	1c	1½c
3 sheets frozen puff pastry, thawed	6	12	18

Serving day

2 eggs

4 t. water

Original recipe yields

4–5 dozen appetizers

Cooking day instructions

In food processor, finely chop mushrooms. Transfer to plate and set aside. Finely chop onions in food processor. In large skillet, melt butter over medium heat. Add mushrooms and onions and cook until juice evaporates, stirring occasionally, about 8 minutes. Add flour, lemon juice, thyme, and Tabasco sauce. Season with salt and pepper to taste. Stir in cream, reduce heat to low, and cook about 2 minutes. Set aside to cool.

Place 1 unfolded pastry sheet on flat surface. Spread evenly with ⅓ of the mushroom mixture. Roll up from both long edges into center, pressing 2 rolls together when they meet in the center. Repeat with remaining 2 pastry sheets. Wrap rolls tightly in plastic wrap and follow with foil. Freeze.

Serving day instructions

Preheat oven to 400 degrees. When rolls are partially thawed, slice into ¼-inch thick slices, using serrated knife. Place, cut side down, on ungreased baking sheet, 1 inch apart. In small bowl, combine eggs and water and whisk to blend. Brush over tops of palmiers and bake 18–20 minutes.

Holiday Fruit Punch

Very festive and delicious at the holidays!

	x3	x6	x9
2 cups cranberry juice	6c	12c	18c
2 cups pineapple juice	6c	12c	18c
6 oz. can frozen lemonade	18oz	36oz	54oz
6 oz. can frozen orange juice	18oz	36oz	54oz
10 oz. package frozen raspberries	30oz	60oz	90oz
1 large lime, sliced	3	6	9
Serving day			
1 quart ginger ale	3qt	6qt	9qt
30 ice cubes	90	180	270

Original recipe yields

4 quarts

Cooking day instructions

Combine all except last two ingredients and place in sealed container in freezer.

Serving day instructions

Remove container from freezer and place frozen mixture in punch bowl. Add ginger ale and ice prior to serving.

Kansas City Hot Wings

A zingy sauce for an old favorite

	x2	x4	x6
4 lbs. chicken wings	8 lbs	16 lbs	24 lbs
½ cup cider vinegar*	¾c	1½c	2¼c
1 T. Tabasco sauce	2T	¼c	¼c + 2T
1 cup Kraft Original Barbecue Sauce	2c	4c	6c

* The measurements for the vinegar in the quantity table are correct. The flavor of acidic ingredients is intensified when a recipe is made in large quantity. The recipe has been adjusted to accommodate this.

Original recipe yields

8–10 servings

Cooking day instructions

Rinse chicken wings in cold water. Mix together vinegar, Tabasco sauce, and barbecue sauce. Place chicken and mixture together in a freezer bag. Freeze, using freezer bag method.

Serving day instructions

Thaw chicken. Preheat oven to 375 degrees. Line a baking pan with foil. Drain chicken wings, reserving remaining sauce. Arrange wings on foil-lined pan and bake for 30 minutes. Remove from heat. Increase temperature of oven to broil. Baste wings with reserved sauce and return to oven. Broil for 30 minutes, turning and basting wings every 5 minutes, until crispy.

Hint

This recipe is great as an appetizer or served as a main dish.

Orange Beef Lettuce Wraps

A wonderful combination of spice, texture, and flavor

	x3	x6	x9
1½ lbs. boneless top sirloin steak	4½ lbs	9 lbs	13½ lbs
1 T. cornstarch	3T	¼c + 2T	½c + 1T
2 T. vegetable oil	⅓c	¾c	1c
⅜ t. crushed red pepper	1⅛t	2¼t	3⅜t
½ cup green onions, thinly sliced	1½c	3c	4½c
1-8 oz. can water chestnuts, drained, then diced	3	6	9
Orange sauce			
3 T. frozen orange juice concentrate, thawed	½c	1c	1½c
3 T. hoisin sauce	½c	1c	1½c
3 T. rice wine vinegar*	½c	1c	1½c
3 T. soy sauce	½c	1c	1½c
1 T. cornstarch	3T	¼c + 2T	½c + 1T
Serving day			
2 heads Boston lettuce leaves, separated			
Shredded carrots			
Diced cucumbers			
Salted peanuts			
Purchased peanut sauce (optional)			

* Rice wine vinegar is usually found in the Asian cooking section of your local grocery store.

Original recipe yields

6 servings

Cooking day instructions

Cut steak into ⅛-inch thick strips. In medium bowl, combine steak and 1 T. cornstarch; toss to coat beef. Set aside. In small bowl, combine orange sauce ingredients; set aside. In large skillet or wok, heat oil and red pepper over medium-high heat until hot. Add beef (half at a time) and stir-fry for 1–2 minutes, until browned on all sides. (Be careful not to overcook.) Add orange sauce mixture, green onions, and water chestnuts. Continue cooking until sauce is thick and bubbly. Remove from heat and cool. Freeze, using freezer bag method.

Serving day instructions

Thaw beef mixture. Reheat in skillet on low until heated through, but do not overcook. To assemble, place a small amount of beef mixture onto center of each lettuce leaf. Top with carrots, cucumbers, peanuts, and peanut sauce as desired, and fold edges of lettuce over into a wrap.

Hint

This recipe may be served as an appetizer or is also great as a main dish.

Substitution

This recipe is also delicious with chicken substituted in place of the steak.

Refreshing Fruit Smoothies

Nutritious and high in flavor

	x2	x4	x6
1 cup vanilla or fruit-flavored yogurt	2c	4c	6c
1 cup fresh or frozen fruit, any combination (strawberries, peaches, bananas, raspberries)	2c	4c	6c
1 cup vanilla ice cream, softened	2c	4c	6c

Serving day

2 cups milk

4–6 ice cubes

Original recipe yields

4–6 servings

Cooking day instructions

Place yogurt, fruit, and ice cream in blender; puree until smooth. Freeze 3 cups of mixture in quart-size freezer bag or 24 oz. freezer container.

Serving day instructions

Place frozen smoothie mixture in jar of blender; add milk and ice cubes. Blend to desired consistency, adding more milk if necessary.

Hints

When making this recipe in larger quantities, purchase the yogurt in economy-size containers.

For an extra nutritional boost, add a scoop of your favorite protein powder.

Santa Fe Hot Dip

Keep this on hand in your freezer for unexpected get-togethers

	x2	x4	x6
16 oz. cream cheese, softened	32oz	64oz	96oz
⅔ cup Parmesan cheese, grated	1⅓c	2⅔c	4c
6 T. mayonnaise	¾c	1½c	2¼c
1-10 oz. pkg. frozen chopped spinach, thawed, drained, squeezed dry	2	4	6
⅔ cup shredded Monterey Jack cheese	1⅓c	2⅔c	4c
½ cup canned green chiles, drained, chopped	1c	2c	3c
2 t. (or more to taste) bottled hot sauce (such as Tabasco sauce)	4t	2T + 2t	4T
½ t. cumin	1t	2t	1T

Original recipe yields

12–14 servings

Cooking day instructions

Beat the cream cheese, Parmesan cheese, and mayonnaise in a mixing bowl until blended. Stir in remaining ingredients. (If you like a spicier dip, add 1 T. finely diced jalapenos or 1 t. cayenne or hot red pepper.) Spoon the cream cheese mixture into a lined, 1-quart soufflé or baking dish. Freeze, using the foil and plastic wrap method.

Serving day instructions

Thaw. Bake at 350 degrees for 20–25 minutes or until brown and bubbly. Serve hot with assorted party crackers, French bread, toasted pita triangles, and/or chips.

South of the Border Queso

Perfect compliment to chips and salsa

	x3	x6	x9
1-32 oz. loaf Velveeta cheese, cut up	3	6	9
1-7 oz. can diced green chiles, drained	3	6	9
2-15 oz. cans Hormel chili, no beans	6	12	18

Original recipe yields

10–15 servings

Cooking day instructions

Mix all ingredients together in medium saucepan. Cook on low heat; continue stirring until cheese is completely melted and ingredients are evenly mixed together. Cool. Freeze in serving-size portions, using freezer bag method.

Serving day instructions

Reheat on stove in medium saucepan over low heat. This dip may also be reheated and kept warm in a Crock-Pot. Dip is best served warm. Serve with chips and salsa.

Strawberry Freeze

Perfect for a backyard picnic

	x2
1 quart fresh strawberries	2qt
2 cups vanilla ice cream, softened	4c
1-3 oz. package strawberry gelatin	2
½ cup boiling water	1c
2 t. lemon juice	4t

Serving day
7 UP (2 liters)
Additional strawberries, for garnish

Original recipe yields

10 servings

Cooking day instructions

In large bowl, mash strawberries and add ice cream. In separate small bowl, dissolve gelatin in the water. Stir in lemon juice. Add to the strawberry mixture and mix well. Freeze mixture in a hard-sided container with lid. This makes it easier to scoop out and serve into glasses using an ice cream scoop. Freeze overnight.

Serving day instructions

Fill serving glass ⅓ to ½ full with frozen mixture. Add 7 UP and stir. Garnish with strawberries and serve.

Hint

Mixture freezes better if placed in several smaller containers.

Breads and Muffins

Chocolate-Orange Crumb Cake
Classic Crumb Cake
Easy No-Knead Rolls
Honey Whole Wheat Bread
Lemon Bread
Orange Sour Cream Loaf
Poppy Seed Pound Cake Muffins
Pumpkin Chocolate Chip Loaf
Quick and Delicious Banana Bread
Sour Cream Muffins
True Blue Muffins
White River Sour Cream Cornbread

Chocolate-Orange Crumb Cake

A perfect blend of chocolate and orange

	x2	x4	x6
2 cups flour	4c	8c	12c
1½ t. baking powder	1T	2T	3T
½ t. baking soda	1t	2t	1T
¼ t. salt	½t	1t	1½t
1 stick unsalted butter	2	4	6
¾ cup sugar	1½c	3c	4½c
1 cup plain yogurt or buttermilk	2c	4c	6c
2 large eggs	4	8	12
1 t. freshly grated orange peel	2t	4t	2T
½ t. vanilla extract	1t	2t	1T

Crumb mixture

	x2	x4	x6
½ cup sugar	1c	2c	3c
¼ cup cocoa powder	½c	1c	1½c
3 T. unsalted butter, cut in small pieces	6T	12T	18T
2 t. freshly grated orange peel	4t	8t	4T

Original recipe yields

One large loaf

Cooking day instructions

Preheat oven to 350 degrees. Mix together flour, baking powder, baking soda, and salt in large bowl. Set aside. Melt butter in medium saucepan over low heat. Remove from heat. Add sugar, yogurt, eggs, orange peel, and vanilla to melted butter. Whisk or stir until well blended.

Put crumb mixture ingredients in small bowl and work until mixture is blended and in small particles. Pour egg mixture over flour mixture and stir just until blended. Spread half this batter in greased 9x5x3 pan and sprinkle with half the crumb mixture. Repeat. Bake until batter is cooked but loaf is still moist (approximately 1 hour). Freeze, using instructions for baked goods.

Serving day instructions

Thaw completely. To maintain freshness, keep cake wrapped airtight in plastic wrap and store at room temperature. Use within one day of removing from freezer.

Classic Crumb Cake

The thick, rich, cinnamony crumbs are irresistible

Crumb Topping	Cake
2 cups flour	2¼ cups flour
½ cup sugar	2¼ t. baking powder
½ cup light brown sugar, packed	½ t. salt
1½ t. grated cinnamon	1¼ cups sugar
1 cup (2 sticks) margarine or butter, softened	½ cup (1 stick) margarine or butter, softened
	3 large eggs
	¾ cup milk
	2 t. vanilla extract

Original recipe yields

2 9-inch crumb cakes, 10 servings each

Cooking day instructions

This recipe should be made in single batches, as it doesn't always rise correctly when doubled.

Preheat oven to 350 degrees. Grease and flour two 9-inch round cake pans.

For crumb topping: In medium bowl, mix flour, sugar, brown sugar, and cinnamon until well blended. With fingertips or pastry blender, work in margarine or butter until evenly distributed. Set aside.

For cake: In another medium bowl, mix flour, baking powder, and salt; set aside. In large bowl, with mixer at low speed, beat sugar with margarine or butter until blended, scraping bowl often. Increase speed to medium; beat until well mixed, about 2 minutes, occasionally scraping bowl. Reduce speed to low; add eggs, 1 at a time, beating well after each addition. Combine milk and vanilla. On low speed, alternately add the flour mixture and milk mixture. Scrape bowl occasionally. Pour batter into pans.

With hand, press crumb topping into very large chunks and evenly sprinkle over batter. Bake cakes 40–45 minutes, until toothpick inserted in center comes out clean. Cool cakes in pans on wire racks 15 minutes. With small spatula, loosen cake from side of pan. Invert onto plate, then immediately invert onto wire rack to cool completely, crumb side up. Freeze, using instructions for baked goods.

Serving day instructions

Thaw completely. Cake can be reheated in microwave or oven until warm.

Easy No-Knead Rolls

These will melt in your mouth

	x3	x6	x9
1 package dry yeast	3 pkgs	6 pkgs	9 pkgs
1 cup warm water	3c	6c	9c
3 eggs	9	18	27
3 T. sugar	½c + 1T	1c + 2T	1½c + 3T
1 t. salt	1T	2T	3T
½ cup cold margarine	1½c	3c	4½c
4 cups flour	12c	24c	36c

Original recipe yields

2½ dozen rolls

Cooking day instructions

Dissolve yeast in warm water. Allow to stand for 5 minutes. In large bowl, beat eggs with electric mixer until light yellow in color. Add sugar, salt, and dissolved yeast to eggs. Stir with spoon to combine. Cut cold margarine into small pieces and gently stir into egg mixture. Add in flour until well combined. Cover bowl with plastic wrap. Let rise in warm place for 2 hours. Shape into dinner rolls and place on greased baking sheets. Cover with a tea towel. Let rise 1 more hour. Preheat oven to 350 degrees and bake until lightly browned. Freeze, using instructions for baked goods.

Serving day instructions

Remove from freezer bag and allow to thaw at room temperature until served.

Honey Whole Wheat Bread

Healthy and so good hot from the oven!

	x2
3½–4 cups flour	7–8c
2½ cups whole wheat flour	5c
2 packages Red Star Dry Yeast	4 pkgs
1 T. salt	2T
1 cup milk	2c
1 cup water	2c
½ cup honey	1c
3 T. vegetable oil	6T
1 egg	2

Original recipe yields

2 large loaves or 3 small loaves

Cooking day instructions

In large bowl, combine 1 cup white flour, whole wheat flour, yeast, and salt; mix well. In saucepan, heat milk, water, honey, and oil until warm; add to flour mixture. Add egg. Blend at low speed until moistened; beat 3 minutes at medium speed. By hand, gradually stir in remaining white flour to make firm dough. Knead on floured surface until smooth and elastic, about 5 minutes. Place in greased bowl, turning to grease top. Cover; let rise in warm place until light and doubled, about 1 hour.

Punch down dough. Divide into 2 parts. On lightly floured surface, roll or pat each half to a 14x17 rectangle. Starting with the shorter side, roll up tightly, pressing dough into roll with each turn. Pinch edges and ends to seal. Place in greased 9x5 loaf pans. Cover and let rise in warm place until light and doubled (about 30 minutes). Preheat oven to 375 degrees and bake for 35–40 minutes until golden brown. Remove from pans and cool. Freeze, using instructions for baked goods.

Serving day instructions

Remove loaf from freezer bag and allow to thaw at room temperature until served.

Lemon Bread

A moist, light bread with a hint of lemon

	x3	x6	x9
1 egg	3	6	9
¾ cup milk	2¼c	4½c	6¾c
¼ cup cooking oil	¾c	1½c	2¼c
1 T. lemon juice	3T	6T	9T
1¾ cups flour	5¼c	10½c	15¾c
¾ cup sugar	2¼c	4½c	6¾c
2 t. baking powder	2T	¼c	6T
2 t. grated lemon peel	2T	¼c	6T
½ t. salt	1½t	1T	4½t

Original recipe yields

One large loaf

Cooking day instructions

Preheat oven to 350 degrees. Beat together egg, milk, oil, and lemon juice. Stir in flour, sugar, baking powder, lemon peel, and salt. Beat well. Pour into greased 9x5 loaf or bread pan. Bake for 50–60 minutes or until toothpick inserted in center comes out clean. Cool in pan 10 minutes. Remove from pan onto wire rack. Freeze, using instructions for baked goods.

Serving day instructions

Remove loaf from freezer bag and allow to thaw at room temperature until served.

Orange Sour Cream Loaf

Perfect for brunch

	x2	x4	x6
1 stick unsalted butter, room temperature	2	4	6
1 cup sugar	2c	4c	6c
2 large eggs	4	8	12
1 T. freshly grated orange peel	2T	¼c	6T
2 cups flour	4c	8c	12c
1 t. baking powder	2t	4t	2T
½ t. baking soda	1t	2t	1T
½ t. salt	1t	2t	1T
1 cup reduced-fat or regular sour cream	2c	4c	6c

Original recipe yields

One loaf

Cooking day instructions

Preheat oven to 350 degrees. Beat butter and sugar with electric mixer on high speed for 5–7 minutes, until pale and fluffy. Scrape the sides of the bowl. Add eggs one at a time, beating after each. Add orange peel. Put flour, baking powder, baking soda, and salt into a bowl. Stir to mix. With mixer on low, add ½ cup of flour mixture. Without waiting for it to mix, add ⅓ of the sour cream. Continue alternating flour and sour cream in the same way until ending with flour. Mix only until well blended.

Spread batter in greased 9x5x3 pan. Bake until pick inserted in center comes out clean, approximately 55 minutes. Cool, then freeze, using instructions for baked goods.

Serving day instructions

Thaw. To maintain freshness, keep loaf wrapped airtight in plastic wrap and store at room temperature. Use within one day of removing from freezer.

Hint

For a variation, make several smaller loaves or muffins.

Poppy Seed Pound Cake Muffins

Make these with your favorite yogurt

	x3	x6	x9
2 cups flour	6c	12c	18c
1 T. poppy seeds	3T	6T	9T
½ t. salt	1½t	1T	4½t
¼ t. baking soda	¾t	1½t	2¼t
1 cup sugar	3c	6c	9c
½ cup butter	1½c	3c	4½c
2 eggs	6	12	18
1 cup plain yogurt	3c	6c	9c
1 t. vanilla	1T	2T	3T

Original recipe yields

12 muffins

Cooking day instructions

Preheat oven to 400 degrees. In small bowl, stir together flour, poppy seeds, salt, and baking soda. In large bowl, cream together sugar and butter. Beat in eggs, one at a time. Beat in yogurt and vanilla until well blended. Stir in flour mixture until moistened thoroughly. Spoon batter into greased muffin tins, and bake for 15–20 minutes or until wooden pick inserted in center comes out clean. Cool muffins on wire rack. Freeze, using instructions for baked goods.

Serving day instructions

Remove muffins from freezer bag and allow to thaw at room temperature until served.

Substitution

For a great variation of this recipe, substitute a flavored yogurt for the plain yogurt. Our favorites are lemon, blueberry, and raspberry.

Pumpkin Chocolate Chip Loaf

Sure to become a fall favorite

	x2	x4	x6
1⅔ cups flour	3⅓c	6⅔c	10c
1 cup sugar	2c	4c	6c
1 T. pumpkin pie spice	2T	¼c	6T
1 t. baking soda	2t	4t	2T
¼ t. baking powder	½t	1t	1½t
dash of salt			
2 eggs	4	8	12
1 cup plain pumpkin	2c	4c	6c
½ cup butter, melted	1c	2c	3c
1 cup chocolate chips	2c	4c	6c

Original recipe yields

1 bundt cake, 2 large loaves, or 24 muffins

Cooking day instructions

Preheat oven to 350 degrees. Mix dry ingredients together in large bowl. Set aside. In small bowl, blend eggs, then add pumpkin and butter. Whisk together. Stir in chocolate chips. Pour wet ingredients into dry ingredients and fold together. Pour into greased baking pans and fill ⅔ full.

Bake 1 hour and 15 minutes for bundt cake, 40–45 minutes for loaves, and 20–25 minutes for muffins. Cool completely. Freeze, using instructions for baked goods.

Serving day instructions

Remove cake, loaf, or muffins from freezer bag and allow to thaw at room temperature until served.

Quick and Delicious Banana Bread

Tried and true

	x3	x6	x9
½ cup butter	1½c	3c	4½c
1 cup sugar	3c	6c	9c
2 eggs	6	12	18
4 large ripe bananas, mashed	12	24	36
1 t. vanilla	1T	2T	3T
1 t. baking soda	1T	2T	3T
1 t. baking powder	1T	2T	3T
2 cups flour	6c	12c	18c
Dash of salt			
1 cup nuts, chopped (optional)	3c	6c	9c

Original recipe yields

4 small loaves or 1 large loaf

Cooking day instructions

Preheat oven to 350 degrees. Cream butter and sugar together. Add eggs and beat. Add bananas and vanilla and beat. Sift together dry ingredients and add gradually to banana mixture, mixing well. Blend in nuts, if desired. Pour into greased and floured loaf pan (pour dough until pan is half full). Bake for 45–50 minutes for a large loaf or 25–30 minutes for small loaves, or until knife inserted in center comes out clean. Freeze, using instructions for baked goods.

Serving day instructions

Remove loaf from freezer bag and allow to thaw at room temperature until served.

Sour Cream Muffins

These melt in your mouth

	x2	x4	x6
3 cups flour	6c	12c	18c
1½ t. baking powder	1T	2T	3T
½ t. baking soda	1t	2t	1T
¼ t. salt	½t	1t	1½t
1½ cups butter	3c	6c	9c
1½ cups sugar	3c	6c	9c
3 eggs	6	12	18
1½ cups sour cream	3c	6c	9c
1½ t. vanilla	1T	2T	3T

Optional topping			
¾ cup brown sugar	1½c	3c	4½c
¾ cup chopped walnuts or pecans	1½c	3c	4½c
1½ t. cinnamon	1T	2T	3T

Original recipe yields

24–30 regular-size muffins

Cooking day instructions

Preheat oven to 350 degrees. Combine dry ingredients and sift. Set aside. In mixer bowl, using medium speed, cream butter and sugar together until light and fluffy. To the creamed mixture, add eggs one at a time, mixing until well combined. Blend in sour cream and vanilla. Add dry ingredients, mixing only until combined. (Don't overmix.)

Spoon muffin batter into muffin tins lined with paper cupcake liners. Fill muffin cups ½ to ⅔ full. (Optional: mix topping ingredients and sprinkle over batter. The muffins are so good even without the topping!)

Bake approximately 15–20 minutes or until light golden brown. To keep muffins moist, test for doneness with toothpick. Do not overbake. Remove muffins from muffin tins and cool on wire rack. Freeze, using instructions for baked goods.

Serving day instructions

Remove muffins from freezer bag and allow to thaw at room temperature until served. Muffins may be reheated just before serving by placing in a preheated 200-degree oven for 5–7 minutes or until heated through.

True Blue Muffins

These complement any quiche

	x2	x4	x6
¼ cup melted butter	½c	1c	1½c
½ cup sugar	1c	2c	3c
1 egg	2	4	6
1¼ cups flour, sifted	2½c	5c	7½c
½ t. salt	1t	2t	1T
2 t. baking powder	4t	8t	4T
¼ cup milk	½c	1c	1½c
¾ cup blueberries—drain and save	1½c	3c	4½c
¼ cup of juice	½c	1c	1½c

Original recipe yields

12 muffins

Cooking day instructions

Preheat oven to 400 degrees. Cream butter and sugar; add egg. Add flour, salt, and baking powder alternating with milk and juice of blueberries. Fold in berries carefully. Bake for 20 minutes. Cool. Freeze, using instructions for baked goods.

Serving day instructions

Remove muffins from freezer bag and allow to thaw at room temperature until served.

White River Sour Cream Cornbread

A perfect complement for Chili Con Carne

	x3	x6	x9
¾ cup flour	2¼c	4½c	6¾c
¼ cup sugar	¾c	1½c	2¼c
1 t. baking powder	1T	2T	3T
½ t. baking soda	1½t	1T	4½t
½ t. salt	1½t	1T	4½t
1¼ cups cornmeal	3¾c	7½c	11¼c
1 egg, slightly beaten	3	6	9
1¼ cups sour cream	3¾c	7½c	11¼c
⅓ cup vegetable oil	1c	2c	3c

Original recipe yields

16 servings

Cooking day instructions

Preheat oven to 400 degrees. Sift together flour, sugar, baking powder, baking soda, and salt in medium bowl. Stir in cornmeal. In separate bowl, combine egg, sour cream, and vegetable oil. Add to dry ingredients until moistened. Pour into greased 8-inch square pan. Bake for 15–18 minutes. For muffins, bake for approximately 12 minutes, or until knife inserted in center comes out clean. Do not overbake. Freeze, using instructions for baked goods.

Serving day instructions

Remove cornbread from freezer bag and allow to thaw at room temperature until served.

Soup's On

Broccoli Cheese Soup
Chicken Noodle Soup
Chicken Tortilla Soup
Chili (New Mexico style)
Chili Con Carne
Colorado White Chili
Cream of Split Pea Soup
French Onion Soup
North Woods Wild Rice Soup
Old-Time Beef Stew
Taco Soup
Tomato and Leek Bisque

Broccoli Cheese Soup

Sure to warm you on a cold winter night

	x3	x6	x9
1 cup carrot, finely chopped	3c	6c	9c
¼ cup celery, finely chopped	¾c	1½c	2¼c
¼ cup onion, finely chopped	¾c	1½c	2¼c
¼ cup green pepper, finely chopped	¾c	1½c	2¼c
½ cup fresh broccoli, cut in small pieces	1½c	3c	4½c
1¾ cups chicken broth	5¼c	10½c	15¾c
2 cups milk	6c	12c	18c
¼ cup flour	¾c	1½c	2¼c
½ t. paprika	1½t	1T	4½t
½ t. salt	1½t	1T	4½t
4 oz. Velveeta cheese	12oz	24oz	36oz
1 cup shredded cheddar cheese	3c	6c	9c
½ cup shredded provolone cheese	1½c	3c	4½c

Original recipe yields

4–6 servings

Cooking day instructions

In stockpot, heat first 6 ingredients to boiling; reduce heat and simmer for 15 minutes or until vegetables are tender. Combine milk, flour, paprika, and salt in a bowl. Add to broth mixture. Cook until thick and bubbly. Add cheese and stir until melted. Freeze, using freezer bag method.

Serving day instructions

Thaw. Heat soup in saucepan until hot. Do not boil. Serve with your favorite bread.

Hint

This soup is excellent with shredded, cooked chicken added.

Chicken Noodle Soup

Serve to warm your soul

	x2	x4	x6
3 lbs. frying chicken, cut up	6 lbs	12 lbs	18 lbs
10 cups water	20c	40c	60c
2 t. chicken bouillon	4t	8t	4T
½ cup onion, chopped	1c	2c	3c
1½ t. salt	1T	2T	3T
½ t. pepper	1t	2t	1T
1 bay leaf	2	4	6
1 cup sliced celery	2c	4c	6c
1 cup thinly sliced carrots	2c	4c	6c
¼ cup chopped onion	½c	1c	1½c

Serving day
2 cups noodles

Original recipe yields

Approximately 7-1½ cup servings

Cooking day instructions

Combine chicken and water. Bring to a boil; reduce heat. Cover and simmer 15 minutes. Skim surface of broth if necessary. Add bouillon granules, ½ cup onion, salt, pepper, and bay leaf. Cover; simmer 35–45 minutes or until chicken is tender. Remove chicken from broth.

Bone chicken and cut up. Skim fat from broth. Return chicken and stir in celery, carrots, and ¼ cup onion. Bring to a boil; reduce heat. Cover and simmer 15 minutes or until carrots are desired tenderness. Soup may be frozen in gallon bags after cooling, using the freezer bag method.

Serving day instructions

Thaw soup until slushy. Place in saucepan. Remove bay leaf and bring to a boil. Drop noodles into boiling soup. Cook uncovered for 5–10 minutes or until noodles are tender.

Chicken Tortilla Soup

Wonderful any time of year

	x3	x6	x9
1 medium onion, chopped	3	6	9
2 cloves garlic, minced	6	12	18
1–2 T. oil for sautéing	3T	⅓c	½c
2 lbs. chicken, baked or boiled, chopped or shredded	6 lbs	12 lbs	18 lbs
14 oz. can diced tomatoes	42oz	84oz	126oz
5 oz. can RO*TEL tomatoes	15oz	30oz	45oz
1-14.5 oz. can beef broth	3	6	9
1-14.5 oz. can chicken broth	3	6	9
1-10 oz. can tomato soup	3	6	9
1½ cans of water (use soup can)	4½	9	13½
1 t. ground cumin	1T	2T	3T
1 t. chili powder	1T	2T	3T
1 t. salt	1T	2T	3T
½ t. lemon-pepper seasoning	1½t	1T	4½t
2 t. Worcestershire sauce	2T	¼c	¼c + 2T
½ t. Tabasco sauce	1½t	1T	4½t

Serving day

Grated cheese for topping

Tortillas cut in 1-inch squares (fried in oil until crispy, or purchase corn tortilla strips or chips)

Avocado, sliced or cubed

Sour cream

Fresh diced tomatoes

Chopped fresh cilantro

Original recipe yields

5–6 servings

Cooking day instructions

Sauté onion and garlic in oil, adding more oil if needed. Add remaining ingredients and simmer 30–35 minutes. Cool. Freeze, using freezer bag method.

Serving day instructions

Thaw. Reheat in stock pot until heated through. Ladle soup into bowls and top with your favorite serving day ingredients.

Chili

New Mexico style green chili

	x2
1½ lb. pork butt or shoulder, diced ¾-inch square (beef roast may be substituted)	3 lbs
1 cup vegetable shortening or canola oil	2c
1½ cups flour	3c
1-27 oz. can green chili pepper strips (or fresh, roasted)	2
1-5 oz. can diced jalapeno peppers or 4 fresh jalapeno peppers, finely chopped	2
1 medium onion, peeled and diced	2
1-27 oz. can whole tomatoes, drained	2
1½ t. ground oregano	1T
1½ t. cumin	1T
1 T. garlic powder or 4–5 cloves fresh garlic	2T
2 quarts water	4 qts

Original recipe yields

A little over 4 quarts

Cooking day instructions

In large kettle, sauté meat in shortening/oil until thoroughly browned. Add flour and stir, cooking until flour is also browned.

In large bowl, mix chilis, peppers, onion, tomatoes, herbs, and spices. Crush together with a potato masher or heavy whisk (for a finer texture, this may be done in a blender or food processor). Add water, mixing well. Stir liquid mixture into the browned pork mixture. After bringing to a boil, reduce heat and simmer 25–30 minutes, stirring occasionally. Cool completely. Freeze, using freezer bag method.

Serving day instructions

Thaw completely. Simmer until heated through and serve. Green chili may also be served with tortillas or used as a sauce to be poured over burritos or other Mexican dishes.

Hint

After freezing and reheating, the vegetable shortening produces a smoother consistency than canola oil.

Chili Con Carne

Be sure to serve with White River Sour Cream Cornbread

	x3	x6	x9
1 lb. ground beef	3 lbs	6 lbs	9 lbs
1 cup onion, chopped	3c	6c	9c
¾ cup green pepper, chopped	2¼c	4½c	6¾c
1 clove garlic, minced	3	6	9
1-16 oz. can tomatoes, cut up	48oz	96oz	144oz
1-16 oz. can dark red kidney beans, drained	48oz	96oz	144oz
1-8 oz. can tomato sauce	24oz	48oz	72oz
2 t. chili powder	2T	4T	6T
½ t. dried basil, crushed	1½t	1T	4½t
½ t. salt	1½t	1T	4½t
¼ t. pepper	¾t	1½t	2¼t

Original recipe yields

4–6 servings

Cooking day instructions

Cook ground beef, onion, green pepper, and garlic until meat is browned. Drain off fat. Stir in undrained tomatoes, kidney beans, tomato sauce, chili powder, basil, salt, and pepper. Bring to boiling; reduce heat. Cover and simmer about 20 minutes longer. Cool, place in gallon bags, and freeze, using freezer bag method.

Serving day instructions

Thaw completely. Simmer until heated through and serve.

Hints

Serve with homemade cornbread or tortillas. Top with grated cheese, sour cream, chopped onions, or your favorite condiments.

Substitutions

Hot or mild green chiles may also be added.

If you prefer a slightly thinner consistency, add more tomato sauce, tomato juice, or V-8 juice.

Colorado White Chili

A healthy, mouth-watering meal sure to bring raves

	x3	x6	x9
1 T. cooking oil	3T	6T	9T
1 medium onion (½ c.), chopped	3	6	9
4 large cloves garlic, minced	12	24	36
1-4.5 oz. can diced green chiles (mild or hot)	3	6	9
1 T. cumin (powder or seed)	3T	6T	9T
2 t. oregano	2T	¼c	6T
½ t. ground red pepper	1½t	1T	4½t
¼ t. ground cloves	¾t	1½t	2¼t
1-15.5 oz. can great northern beans (do not drain)	3	6	9
1-15.5 oz. can sweet corn (or frozen)	3	6	9
2 cups cooked chicken, chopped	6c	12c	18c
5 cups chicken broth	15c	30c	45c

Serving day

Shredded Monterey Jack cheese

Sour cream

Tortilla chips

Original recipe yields

6–8 servings

Cooking day instructions

In a large pan (or Dutch oven), combine oil, onion, garlic, and green chiles. Sauté until tender, but do not brown. Stir in spices, beans, corn, chopped chicken, and chicken broth. Cook and stir until heated through. Adjust seasonings to taste. Cool chili completely. Freeze, using freezer bag method.

Serving day instructions

Thaw completely. Simmer until heated through. Serve in bowls with cheese, sour cream, and tortilla chips. For extra "kick," garnish with jalapeno slices.

Hint

If using dry beans: To prepare dry beans, rinse 1 lb. beans. In Dutch oven, combine beans and 4 cups water. Bring to boiling; reduce heat. Cover and let stand for 1 hour. (Or soak beans in cold water overnight in a covered pan.) Drain and rinse beans. Combine beans, ¼ c. onion, chicken broth, and garlic. Bring to boiling; reduce heat. Cover and simmer for about 1 hour or until beans are tender. Then add remaining ingredients, and continue following cooking day instructions above.

Substitution

Reduced-sodium chicken broth can be used.

Cream of Split Pea Soup

A smooth, creamy version of an old favorite

	x2	x4	x6
2 cups split peas, washed	4c	8c	12c
4½ cups boiling water	9c	18c	27c
½ cup diced celery	1c	2c	3c
½ cup diced carrots	1c	2c	3c
1 onion, chopped	2	4	6
2 t. salt	4t	8t	4T

Serving day

2½ cups milk

1 cup chopped ham or corned beef (optional)

Original recipe yields

6–8 servings

Cooking day instructions

Combine all ingredients and simmer slowly until peas are soft, 45 minutes or more, stirring occasionally. Process in blender. Freeze, using freezer bag method.

Serving day instructions

Add milk and chopped ham or corned beef (optional) to the soup. Blend thoroughly and heat through. Adjust seasonings as desired.

French Onion Soup

Serve with salad and crusty rolls for a complete meal

	x3	x6	x9
4 large yellow onions	12	24	36
2 T. butter	6T	¾c	1c + 2T
1 T. flour	3T	6T	½c + 1T
6 cups beef broth	18c	36c	54c
¼ t. salt	¾t	1½t	2¼t
¼ t. pepper	¾t	1½t	2¼t

Serving day

6 slices French bread

¾ cup Swiss cheese, grated

¼ cup fresh Parmesan cheese, grated

Original recipe yields

6 servings

Cooking day instructions

Peel onions and slice thinly. Separate into rings. Sauté onion rings in hot butter in skillet until softened, and lightly stir in flour. Heat beef broth in stockpot until simmering. Add onions to hot broth. Cover stockpot and simmer for 20 minutes. Add salt and pepper. Freeze, using freezer bag method.

Serving day instructions

Thaw completely. Gently reheat soup over low heat, then ladle into individual soup dishes. Preheat broiler. Place a slice of French bread on top of each filled soup bowl. Sprinkle with combined cheeses. Place bowls on a cookie sheet and brown cheese under broiler for 3 minutes, until cheese is bubbling.

North Woods Wild Rice Soup

A hearty, delicious soup!

	x3	x6	x9
½ lb. bacon	1½ lbs	3 lbs	4½ lbs
½ onion, diced	1½	3	4½
½ cup celery, chopped	1½c	3c	4½c
¼ cup butter or margarine	¾c	1½c	2¼ c
3 T. flour	½c + 1T	1c + 2T	1¾c
½ t. salt	1½t	1T	4½t
½ t. thyme	1½t	1T	4½t
½ t. paprika	1½t	1T	4½t
1½ cups cooked chicken breast, shredded or cubed	4½c	9c	13½c
1-10 oz. can chicken broth	3	6	9
1 T. Worcestershire sauce	3T	⅓c	½c
2 T. cooking sherry	⅓c	¾c	1c + 2T
1 cup milk	3c	6c	9c
1½ cups half-and-half	4½c	9c	13½c
1½ cups cooked wild rice	4½c	9c	13½c

Original recipe yields

6 large bowls of soup

Cooking day instructions

Fry, drain, and crumble bacon; set aside. Sauté onion and celery in butter until tender. Stir in flour, salt, thyme, and paprika. Heat until bubbly. Add cooked chicken, chicken broth, Worcestershire sauce, sherry, milk, and half-and-half, stirring until thickened. Cool. Fold in rice and bacon. Freeze, using freezer bag method.

Serving day instructions

Heat soup in saucepan until bubbly. Serve with your favorite bread.

Hint

If using prepackaged wild rice, do not add any seasoning pouches that may be included in the package to this soup.

Old-Time Beef Stew

For a hassle-free meal, make in the Crock-Pot

	x3	x6	x9
2 lbs. beef cubes (stew meat)	6 lbs	12 lbs	18 lbs
1 T. oil	3T	6T	9T
4 cups boiling water	12c	24c	36c
1 T. lemon juice	3T	6T	9T
1 t. Worcestershire sauce	1T	2T	3T
1 clove garlic, minced	3	6	9
1 onion, sliced	3	6	9
1 T. salt	3T	6T	9T
2 bay leaves	6	12	18
½ t. pepper	1½t	1T	1½T
1 t. sugar	1T	2T	3T
½ t. paprika	1½t	1T	1½T
Dash of allspice			

Serving day

1 lb. carrots, chopped

3–4 potatoes, chopped

1–2 cups frozen peas

Original recipe yields

6–8 servings

Cooking day instructions

Brown meat in oil. Add rest of ingredients and cook 1–2 hours, until meat is tender. Freeze, using freezer bag method.

Serving day instructions

Thaw completely and place stew in stockpot. Add vegetables and simmer 1–2 hours, until vegetables are tender. If desired, some of the liquid may be thickened with flour and poured over the meat and vegetables.

Taco Soup

A great warm-up dinner on a chilly day

	x3	x6	x9
1 lb. ground beef	3 lbs	6 lbs	9 lbs
1 onion, chopped	3	6	9
1 package taco seasoning	3 pkgs	6 pkgs	9 pkgs
1-15 oz. can diced tomatoes	3	6	9
1-15 oz. can corn	3	6	9
1-15 oz. can kidney beans	3	6	9
1-15 oz. can pinto beans	3	6	9
1-15 oz. can water	3	6	9

Serving day

Fritos corn chips

Original recipe yields

4–5 servings

Cooking day instructions

Brown ground beef and onion in skillet; drain. Place ground beef mixture, taco seasoning, tomatoes, corn, kidney beans, pinto beans, and water in pan on stove. Simmer for 30–40 minutes. Freeze, using freezer bag method.

Serving day instructions

Thaw soup and heat thoroughly in saucepan. Place in bowls with Fritos chips on top.

Hints

Soup may also be served with cheese and sour cream on top. It's excellent when served with cornbread.

Tomato and Leek Bisque

An elegant start to a holiday dinner

	x3	x6	x9
¼ cup olive oil	¾c	1½c	2¼c
8 cups chopped leeks, white and pale green parts only (about 3–4 leeks)	24c	48c	72c
2 stalks celery, chopped	6	12	18
1 clove garlic, chopped	3	6	9
2-14.5 oz. cans whole peeled tomatoes	6	12	18
1-14.5 oz. can chicken broth	3	6	9
¾ cup dry white wine	2¼c	4½c	6¾c
1 T. fresh lemon juice	3T	6T	9T
1½ T. chopped fresh basil leaves or 2 t. dried basil leaves	4½T (2T)	9T (4T)	¾c (6T)
½ t. salt	1½t	1T	4½t
¼ t. ground white pepper	¾t	1½t	2¼t

Serving day

¾ cup whipping cream

Original recipe yields

About 9 cups soup

Cooking day instructions

In heavy pan, heat oil, leeks, celery, and garlic over medium-high heat; cook 8–10 minutes or until leeks are soft. Add tomatoes, chicken broth, wine, and lemon juice. Bring mixture to a boil; reduce heat to medium-low, cover, and simmer 30 minutes. Remove from heat; add fresh or dry basil, salt, and white pepper. Puree soup mixture in food processor or blender until smooth. Freeze in gallon or quart bags, using freezer bag method.

Serving day instructions

Thaw; heat through over low heat, stirring occasionally; add cream and simmer about 10 minutes or until thickened. *Do not boil*. Garnish with basil. Serve warm.

Hints

Serve with fresh, hot bread or muffins.

   This soup also makes a great first course or soup course for a dinner party or special gathering.

Substitutions

Light cream (half-and-half) or milk may be used instead of whipping cream.

Poultry

Buttermilk Herb Chicken Breasts
Cheesy Chicken Bundles
Chicken à la King
Chicken Breasts in Phyllo
Chicken Breasts Stuffed with Pesto Butter
Chicken Cacciatore
Chicken Cilantro Enchiladas
Chicken Enchiladas
Chicken Lelani
Chicken Parisienne
Chicken Pot Pie
Chicken in Raspberry Sauce
Chicken Wellington
Cranberry Chicken
Elegant Chicken Roll
Grilled Turkey Breast with Peanut Sauce
Hawaiian Chicken
Honey Pecan Chicken
Italian Stuffed Chicken Breasts
Lemon Glazed Chicken Breasts
Orange Teriyaki Chicken
Oriental Sesame Chicken Strips
Pecan Stuffed Chicken Breasts
Polynesian Chicken Bundles
Teriyaki Chicken (or Steak)
Tropical Chicken Ribbons
Turkey Picante Pie

Buttermilk Herb Chicken Breasts

As attractive as they are delicious

	x2	x4	x6
1 cup buttermilk	2c	4c	6c
1 T. Dijon mustard	2T	¼c	¼c +2T
1 T. honey	2T	¼c	¼c +2T
1 T. fresh rosemary, finely chopped	2T	¼c	¼c +2T
½ t. dried thyme	1t	2t	1T
½ t. dried sage	1t	2t	1T
½ t. dried marjoram	1t	2t	1T
½ t. pepper	1t	2t	1T
1 t. salt	2t	4t	2T
8 boneless split chicken breasts	16	32	48

Original recipe yields

8 servings

Cooking day instructions

Mix together buttermilk with mustard, honey, and seasonings. Place chicken breasts in freezer bag. Pour marinade over chicken breasts. Freeze, using freezer bag method.

Serving day instructions

Thaw chicken, discarding marinade. Grill over medium heat until chicken is tender and juices run clear.

Hint

For a "kid-friendly" version, after grilling, cut chicken breasts into strips. Serve with a ranch-dressing dipping sauce.

Cheesy Chicken Bundles

Kids will love these!

	x3	x6	x9
1 cup bread crumbs	3c	6c	9c
½ cup cheddar cheese, grated	1½c	3c	4½c
½ cup fresh Parmesan cheese, grated	1½c	3c	4½c
1 t. salt	1T	2T	3T
¼ t. pepper	¾t	1½t	2¼t
6 boneless chicken breasts	18	36	54
½ cup butter, melted	1½c	3c	4½c

Serving day

2 T. butter, melted

¼ cup fresh Parmesan cheese, grated

Original recipe yields

6 servings

Cooking day instructions

Mix together bread crumbs, cheeses, salt, and pepper. Dip chicken pieces in melted butter, then in cheese mixture. Tuck sides of chicken breast under to form individual bundles. To freeze, wrap each bundle in plastic wrap, and then place in freezer bags.

Serving day instructions

Thaw, then place chicken bundles in large, shallow baking dish. Melt remaining 2 T. butter and pour over bundles. Sprinkle with ¼ cup Parmesan cheese. Bake uncovered at 350 degrees approximately 1 hour, until chicken is crispy.

Chicken à la King

Sooooo good served over puff pastry shells

	x3	x6	x9
4 oz. mushrooms, sliced	12oz	24oz	36oz
⅔ cup green pepper, chopped	2c	4c	6c
½ cup margarine or butter	1½c	3c	4½c
½ cup flour	1½c	3c	4½c
¼ t. pepper	¾t	1½t	2¼t
2 t. chicken bouillon	2T	4T	6T
2 cups milk	6c	12c	18c
1 cup water	3c	6c	9c
2½ cups cooked chicken, cut up	7½c	15c	22½c
4 oz. jar pimiento, drained	12oz	24oz	36oz

Serving day

Pastry shells

Original recipe yields

6 servings

Cooking day instructions

In large skillet over medium-high heat, cook mushrooms and green pepper in margarine until green pepper is crisp-tender; remove from heat. Lightly spoon flour into measuring cup; level off. Stir in flour and pepper. Cook over low heat until mixture is smooth and bubbly, stirring constantly. Stir in bouillon granules, milk, and water. Bring to a boil. Boil and stir 1 minute. Stir in chicken and pimiento. Cook until thoroughly heated. Freeze, using freezer bag method.

Serving day instructions

Thaw and reheat in saucepan. Serve over puff pastry shells or toast.

Chicken Breasts in Phyllo

An easy and elegant dinner entrée sure to bring raves

	x3
1½ cups mayonnaise	4½c
1 cup green onion, chopped	3c
⅓ cup lemon juice	1c
2 cloves garlic, minced	6
2 t. dry tarragon	2T
12 chicken breast halves, boned and skinned	36
Salt and pepper to taste	
24 sheets phyllo dough*	72
1½ cups butter, melted	4½c
⅓ cup Parmesan cheese, freshly grated	1c

* Phyllo dough can be found in the refrigerated or freezer section of most grocery stores.

Original recipe yields

12 servings

Cooking day instructions

Combine first 5 ingredients to make sauce. Lightly sprinkle chicken breasts with salt and pepper. Place 2 sheets of phyllo on working surface. Quickly brush each sheet with melted butter (about 2 t.) and stack on top of each other. Spread about 1½ T. of sauce on each side of chicken. Place breast in one corner of buttered phyllo sheets. Fold corner over breast, then fold sides over, and roll breast up in the sheets to form a package. Place in ungreased baking dish. Repeat with remaining chicken breasts and phyllo sheets. Brush packets with remaining butter and sprinkle with Parmesan cheese. Wrap each chicken breast in plastic wrap and place in a freezer bag.

Serving day instructions

Thaw completely before baking. Bake at 375 degrees in ungreased baking dish for 45–50 minutes or until golden. Serve immediately.

Substitution

Cream cheese may be used in place of mayonnaise.

Chicken Breasts Stuffed with Pesto Butter

An upscale entrée for guests

	x2	x4	x6
6 boned chicken breast halves	12	24	36
½ cup fresh basil leaves, washed and dried*	1c	2c	3c
¼ cup freshly grated Parmesan cheese	½c	1c	1½c
1 garlic clove, minced	2	4	6
½ cup butter (1 cube), room temperature	1c	2c	3c
⅓ cup flour (seasoned with salt & pepper)	⅔c	1⅓c	2c
1 egg, well beaten	2	4	6
¾ cup fine dry bread crumbs	1½c	3c	4½c

Serving day

2 T. butter

2 T. olive oil

* Fresh basil leaves (stored in bags) are usually found in the produce section of the grocery store.

Original recipe yields

6 servings

Cooking day instructions

Flatten chicken breasts to ⅛-inch thickness (see "Get to Know Your Butcher" on page 16). In food processor or blender, combine basil, cheese, and garlic. Mix until a thick paste is formed. Add butter and blend. On a piece of waxed paper or plastic wrap, shape into a 3-inch square. Chill until firm. (To quick-chill, place in freezer for 10–20 minutes.) Slice chilled square of pesto butter into 6 sticks, approximately ½ inch wide and 3 inches long.

Lay out a flattened chicken breast. Place a stick of pesto butter on the larger side of the meat. Fold the remaining side over the butter, then fold under the two ends. Press meat together on all sides to securely enclose butter.

Using 3 separate plates, place seasoned flour in one, beaten egg in another, and bread crumbs in the third. Dredge rolled chicken breast in flour and shake off excess. Dip into egg, then roll in bread crumbs. Firmly pat bread crumbs onto chicken. Refrigerate chicken rolls for at least 1 hour to allow crumbs to adhere. At this point, chicken rolls may be frozen. Wrap each chicken breast in plastic wrap, and place in freezer bags.

Serving day instructions

Unwrap chicken rolls and put on plate in refrigerator. Thaw completely. In large sauté pan, heat butter and olive oil on medium to medium high. Sauté chicken for about 10–15 minutes, turning chicken until golden brown on all sides. Place in lightly greased baking dish and bake in preheated, 350-degree oven for approximately 40–45 minutes or until meat is white all the way through. (Be careful not to overbake, as chicken becomes tough.)

Chicken Cacciatore

A savory Crock-Pot recipe

	x2	x4	x6
2 medium onions, sliced thin	4	8	12
2 cloves garlic, minced	4	8	12
1-15oz. can diced tomatoes	2	4	6
1-8oz. can tomato sauce	2	4	6
1 t. salt	2t	4t	2T
¼ t. pepper	½t	1t	1½t
2 t. oregano	4t	8t	4T
½ t. basil	1t	2t	1T
½ t. celery seed	1t	2t	1T
1 bay leaf	2	4	6
¼ cup white wine	½c	1c	1½c
6 boned chicken breasts	12	24	36

Serving day

Pasta

Original recipe yields

6 servings

Cooking day instructions

Mix together onions, garlic, tomatoes, tomato sauce, salt, pepper, herbs, and wine. Place this mixture together with chicken breasts in a freezer bag. Freeze, using freezer bag method.

Serving day instructions

Place in Crock-Pot and cook on low 6–8 hours or on high 2½–4 hours. Serve over pasta.

Chicken Cilantro Enchiladas

Sure to satisfy your craving for Mexican

	x3	x6	x9
2 lbs. boneless, skinless chicken breasts	6 lbs	12 lbs	18 lbs
2 cups water	6c	12c	18c
1 onion, diced	3	6	9
1 clove garlic, minced	3	6	9
2–3 sprigs fresh cilantro	6–9	12–18	18–27
1⅓ cups chicken broth	4c	8c	12c
2-10 oz. cans mild enchilada sauce	6	12	18
4 cups grated Monterey Jack cheese	12c	24c	36c
8 green onions, sliced	24	48	72
2 T. chopped cilantro leaves	⅓c	¾c	1c
½ t. salt	1½t	1T	4½t
¼ t. pepper	¾t	1½t	2¼t
Tabasco sauce, to taste			
10 corn tortillas	30	60	90

Original recipe yields

10 servings

Cooking day instructions

Bring chicken breasts to boil in water with onion, garlic, and cilantro sprigs. Reduce heat and simmer until chicken is tender, about 10 minutes. Remove chicken from broth and cool; shred meat; strain broth. Add 1⅓ cups chicken broth to enchilada sauce; set aside.

For filling, combine chicken, 2 cups cheese, green onions, and chopped cilantro leaves with salt, pepper, and Tabasco sauce to taste. Add 1 cup enchilada sauce/broth mixture to moisten filling.

To assemble, warm tortillas on hot skillet or griddle until flexible, turning once. Dip each corn tortilla in enchilada sauce mixture until coated on each side and lay flat. Fill with 2–3 T. chicken filling and roll tortilla. Place filled tortillas, seam side down, in lined 9x13 baking dish. Spoon remaining sauce

▶

over filled tortillas; sprinkle with remaining 2 cups cheese. Freeze, using foil and plastic wrap method.

Serving day instructions

Thaw completely. Bake at 350 degrees for 25–35 minutes, until sauce bubbles and cheese is melted. Top with your choice of lettuce, tomato, sour cream, and sliced avocados.

Chicken Enchiladas

Chicken enchiladas baked in a cheesy white sauce

	x3	x6	x9
1 cup onion, chopped	3c	6c	9c
½ cup green pepper, chopped	1½c	3c	4½c
2 T. butter or margarine	6T	¾c	1c + 2T
2 cups cooked chicken or turkey	6c	12c	18c
1-4 oz. can green chili peppers, chopped	3	6	9
3 T. butter or margarine	9T	1c + 2T	1½c + 3T
¼ cup flour	¾c	1½c	2¼c
1 t. ground coriander	1T	2T	3T
¾ t. salt	2¼t	4½t	6¾t
2½ cups chicken broth	7½c	15c	22½c
1 cup sour cream	3c	6c	9c
6 oz. (1½ cups) Monterey Jack cheese, shredded	18oz	36oz	54oz
12 6-inch tortillas	36	72	108

Original recipe yields

12 enchiladas

Cooking day instructions

Cook onion and green pepper in 2 T. butter until tender. Combine onion mixture in a bowl with chicken and chili peppers; set aside.

For sauce, melt 3 T. butter and stir in flour, coriander, and salt. Stir in chicken broth all at once; cook and stir until thickened and bubbly. Cook and stir 1–2 minutes more. Remove from heat; stir in sour cream and ½ cup of cheese. Stir ½ cup of sauce into chicken mixture.

Dip each tortilla into remaining sauce to soften; fill each with about ¼ cup of chicken mixture. Roll up. Arrange rolls in a lined baking dish for freezing. Pour remaining sauce over enchiladas and sprinkle with remaining cheese. Freeze, using the foil and plastic wrap method.

Serving day instructions

Thaw completely. Bake uncovered at 350 degrees for about 25 minutes or until bubbly.

Chicken Lelani

A chicken dish with a Polynesian flair

	x3	x6	x9
4 large boneless chicken breasts, cooked	12	24	36
2 cans cream of celery soup	6	12	18
2 cups evaporated milk	6c	12c	18c
2 cups minced celery	6c	12c	18c
2 t. minced onion	2T	4T	6T
½ t. Worcestershire sauce	1½t	1T	4½t
1 cup blanched and slivered almonds	3c	6c	9c
2 cups Chinese chow mein noodles (crunchy)	6c	12c	18c

Original recipe yields

6 servings

Cooking day instructions

Cut chicken into bite-size pieces. Blend soup and milk together. Add celery, onions, Worcestershire sauce, and ¾ cup almonds; stir together.

Layer Chinese noodles and chicken alternately in a lined baking dish. Pour sauce over layers. Make a ring around top of casserole with remainder of almonds. Freeze, using foil and plastic wrap method.

Serving day instructions

Thaw completely and bake at 350 degrees for 45 minutes.

Chicken Parisienne

Crock-Pot dish with a French twist

	x2	x4	x6
½ cup white wine	1c	2c	3c
1-10 oz. can cream of mushroom soup	2	4	6
½ cup mushrooms, sliced	1c	2c	3c
¼ cup flour	½c	1c	1½c
1 cup sour cream	2c	4c	6c
6 boned chicken breasts	12	24	36

Serving day

Salt and pepper

Paprika

Original recipe yields

6 servings

Cooking day instructions

Mix wine, soup, and mushrooms together. Stir flour into sour cream and add to soup mixture. Place mixture together with chicken in freezer bag. Freeze, using freezer bag method.

Serving day instructions

Place chicken and sauce in Crock-Pot. Sprinkle salt, pepper, and paprika over top. Cover and cook on low for 6–8 hours.

Hint

Serve with pasta or potatoes.

Chicken Pot Pie

Incredible flavor!

	x3	x6	x9
1-10 oz. package frozen peas and carrots	30oz	60oz	90oz
½ cup onion, chopped	1½c	3c	4½c
½ cup fresh mushrooms, chopped	1½c	3c	4½c
¼ cup butter or margarine	¾c	1½c	2¼c
⅓ cup flour	1c	2c	3c
½ t. salt	1½t	1T	4½t
¼ t. sage	¾t	1½t	2¼t
⅛ t. pepper	⅜t	¾t	1⅛t
2 cups water	6c	12c	18c
¾ cup milk	2¼c	4½c	6¾c
1 T. chicken bouillon	3T	6T	9T
3 cups cooked chicken (or turkey)	9c	18c	27c
¼ cup chopped pimiento	¾c	1½c	2¼c
¼ cup snipped parsley	¾c	1½c	2¼c

Serving day

Double pie crust

Original recipe yields

1 deep dish or 2 standard 9-inch pies

Cooking day instructions

Cook peas and carrots according to package directions; drain. Cook onion and mushrooms in butter or margarine until tender but not brown. Stir in flour, salt, sage, and pepper. Add water, milk, and bouillon granules all at once. Cook and stir until thickened and bubbly. Cook and stir 1–2 minutes more. Stir in drained cooked vegetables, chicken or turkey, pimiento, and parsley; heat until bubbly. Freeze, using freezer bag method.

Serving day instructions

Thaw completely. Roll out bottom pie crust and place in 9-inch pie pan. Place chicken mixture in pie dish; top with upper crust. Bake in pie shell in 400-degree oven for 25–30 minutes or until golden brown.

Hint

To determine how much to freeze in each bag, measure mixture directly into pie plate to be used. We use approximately 3½ cups per pie.

Chicken in Raspberry Sauce

An elegant dish for friends or family

	x3	x6	x9
½ cup raspberry preserves (fruit-only type)	1½c	3c	4½c
½ cup frozen pineapple juice concentrate, thawed	1½c	3c	4½c
½ cup soy sauce	1½c	3c	4½c
2 T. rice wine vinegar	6T	¾c	1c + 2T
½ t. chili powder	1½t	1T	4½t
½ t. curry powder	1½t	1T	4½t
½ t. garlic powder	1½t	1T	4½t
¼ cup fresh raspberries, mashed	¾c	1½c	2¼c
6 boneless, skinless chicken breasts	18	36	54

Serving day

¼ cup fresh raspberries

Original recipe yields

6 servings

Cooking day instructions

Combine preserves, juice concentrate, soy sauce, vinegar, chili powder, curry powder, garlic powder, and mashed raspberries. Place raspberry mixture together with chicken breasts in freezer bag and seal bag securely. Freeze, using freezer bag method.

Serving day instructions

Thaw chicken mixture completely and place sauce and chicken in large baking dish. Bake covered at 350 degrees for 30–40 minutes. Remove from oven, transfer chicken to serving platter, and top with pan juices. Garnish with fresh raspberries.

Hint

If fresh raspberries are not available, frozen raspberries may be substituted.

Chicken Wellington

A classic!

	x3	x6	x9
4 boneless, skinless chicken breasts	12	24	36
2 T. butter	6T	¾c	1c + 2T
3 oz. cream cheese, softened	9oz	18oz	27oz
4 oz. can mushrooms, drained	12oz	24oz	36oz
2 T. chopped green onions	6T	¾c	1c + 2T
¼ t. salt	¾t	1½t	2¼t
⅛ t. pepper	⅜t	¾t	1⅛t
1-10 oz. can refrigerated crescent rolls or phyllo dough sheets	3	6	9

Serving day

1 egg, beaten

Sauce

3 T. butter

1 T. green onion

2½ T. flour

1½ c. milk

½ t. salt

¾ cup cheese or 2 oz. mushrooms

Original recipe yields

4 servings

Cooking day instructions

Flatten chicken breasts to ⅛-inch thickness (see "Get to Know Your Butcher" on page 16). Pan fry in butter until almost white throughout. Combine cream cheese, mushrooms, green onion, salt, and pepper. Place 2 T. of mix in center of each chicken piece. Roll up chicken breast and place in center of roll or phyllo dough. Wrap dough around and seal. To freeze, wrap each breast in plastic wrap, then place in freezer bags.

Serving day instructions

Thaw, then place seam down on ungreased cookie sheet. Brush with egg. Bake at 375 degrees for 20–30 minutes. While baking, make sauce. Melt butter and sauté onion until tender. Blend in flour; gradually add milk and salt. Cook until thickened. Add mushrooms or cheese. Serve over chicken.

Cranberry Chicken

Surprisingly delicious!

	x3	x6	x9
8 oz. Catalina dressing	24oz	48oz	72oz
1 pkg. dry onion soup mix	3 pkgs	6 pkgs	9 pkgs
1-1 lb. can whole-berry cranberry sauce	3	6	9
4 boned chicken breasts	12	24	36

Original recipe yields

4 servings

Cooking day instructions

Mix together dressing, onion soup mix, and cranberry sauce. Place chicken and mixture together in a freezer bag. Freeze, using freezer bag method.

Serving day instructions

Thaw completely. Place chicken with cranberry sauce in greased baking dish, and bake uncovered at 350 degrees for 1–1½ hours.

Elegant Chicken Roll

Melts in your mouth!

	x3	x6	x9
4 boneless, skinless chicken breast halves	12	24	36
1 cup ground beef	3c	6c	9c
2 T. fresh chives, chopped	6T	¾c	1c + 2T
¼ t. salt	¾t	1½t	2¼t
⅛ t. pepper	⅜t	¾t	1⅛t
8 oz. garlic cream cheese	24oz	48oz	72oz

Serving day

2 T. honey

Original recipe yields

One large roll

Cooking day instructions

Place chicken breasts, side by side, between two pieces of plastic wrap. Beat with a meat mallet until breasts are ½ inch thick and joined together in one long row, forming a rectangle.

Place ground beef in large skillet and cook until just brown. Add fresh chives, salt, and pepper. Cool.

Spread chicken with cream cheese. Top with beef mixture, spreading it evenly over cream cheese. Starting at the narrow end, roll up chicken tightly to form a log. Freeze, using the foil and plastic wrap method, placing in a loaf pan to shape while freezing.

Serving day instructions

Allow chicken roll to thaw in loaf pan. Preheat oven to 375 degrees. When roll is thawed, brush with honey and bake for one hour. Remove from pan and slice thinly.

Grilled Turkey Breast with Peanut Sauce

This is a much-requested recipe for entertaining and always gets rave reviews

	x3	x6	x9
½ cup chunky peanut butter	1½c	3c	4½c
¼ cup soy sauce*	¾c	1½c	2¼c
¼ cup sesame oil*	¾c	1½c	2¼c
1 large garlic clove, minced	3	6	9
1 T. sugar	3T	¼c	¼c + 2T
¼ cup cider vinegar	¾c	1½c	2¼c
4½ t. oriental hot pepper oil*	¼c	½c	¾c
1 cup sour cream (low fat can be used)	3c	6c	9c
3–4 T. milk (as needed)	½–¾c	1–1½c	1½–2c
3 lbs. turkey breast tenderloins, boned, or cut whole breast into 1½-inch thick serving portions	8–9 lbs	16–18 lbs	24–26 lbs

*Can be found in much larger quantities in Asian markets or some larger grocery stores.

Original recipe yields

6–8 servings

Cooking day instructions

To make peanut sauce, combine all ingredients except milk and turkey breast and mix well. Thin sauce with a little milk if necessary to make the consistency of softly whipped cream. Set aside.

If skin is still intact, gently loosen and remove skin and any fat from turkey breasts. Cover with plastic wrap and flatten with a mallet or rolling pin to approximately 1 inch thick. Place turkey in freezer bag and pour half the peanut sauce over breasts. Refrigerate for several hours if serving that day.

To freeze for later use, place turkey breasts in freezer bag; pour half of sauce over turkey, reserving the remainder for separate use. Place reserved sauce in separate bag and clearly label. Keep bags together in freezer.

Serving day instructions

Thaw turkey breasts and discard peanut sauce that turkey was marinated in. Also thaw bag of reserved peanut sauce. Prepare outdoor grill or indoor broiler. Grill turkey breast tenderloins over a moderately hot fire for 15 minutes per side or until a slit in the middle reveals opaque meat. If broiling indoors, place turkey breasts 6 inches from broiler. They may need to be turned more often to prevent burning. Check meat for doneness.

Serve with reserved peanut sauce, brought to room temperature and whisked to a smooth consistency. To serve the sauce hot, heat on low or place in the microwave for 1–2 minutes; do not boil, as sauce may separate.

For a sweeter peanut sauce, more sugar may be added at this point. (Start with ½ t. until desired sweetness is reached.) Or for a spicier sauce, add ⅛–¼ t. ground red pepper (cayenne) to sauce, whisk in completely, and taste, adding more for spicier sauce.

Hint

This dish can also be served cold or at room temperature for picnics, potlucks, or barbecues. The flavor is wonderful hot or cold.

Substitution

Chicken breasts may be substituted for turkey tenderloins.

Hawaiian Chicken

Make in the Crock–Pot and serve over rice

	x3	x6	x9
6 lbs. boneless, skinless chicken breast halves	18 lbs	36 lbs	54 lbs
2-16 oz. cans pineapple slices, drained	6	12	18
2-15 oz. cans mandarin oranges, drained	6	12	18
¼ cup cornstarch	¾c	1½c	2¼c
½ cup brown sugar	1½c	3c	4½c
¼ cup soy sauce	¾c	1½c	2¼c
¼ cup lemon juice*	½c	1c	1½c
1 t. salt	1T	2T	3T
1 t. ground ginger	1T	2T	3T
½ t. ground red pepper	1½t	1T	4½t

Serving day

Steamed rice

Toasted almonds

Green pepper chunks (optional)

* The measurements for the lemon juice in the quantity table are correct. The flavor of acidic ingredients is intensified when a recipe is made in large quantity. The recipe has been adjusted to accommodate this.

Original recipe yields

8–10 servings

Cooking day instructions

Place chicken in freezer bag. Mix together fruit, cornstarch, sugar, soy sauce, lemon juice, salt, ginger, and ground red pepper. Pour over the chicken in bag. Freeze, using freezer bag method.

Serving day instructions

Thaw chicken mixture. Place in Crock-Pot, cover, and cook on low for 4–5 hours or on high for 2–3 hours. Add green pepper to Crock-Pot one hour before serving, if desired. To serve, spoon over steamed rice and top with toasted almonds.

Honey Pecan Chicken

The honey cream sauce creates a succulent dish

	x3	x6	x9
6 boneless, skinless chicken breast halves	18	36	54
Marinade			
½ cup olive oil	1½c	3c	4½c
2 t. fresh thyme, minced	2T	¼c	¼c + 2T
3 cloves garlic, minced	9	18	27
½ t. salt	1½t	1T	4½t
¼ t. pepper	¾t	1½t	2¼t
Honey cream sauce			
2 T. butter	6T	¾c	1c + 2T
1 T. shallots, minced	3T	⅓c	½c
1 cup orange juice	3c	6c	9c
¼ cup whiskey	¾c	1½c	2¼c
1 cup whipping cream	3c	6c	9c
2 T. honey	6T	¾c	1c + 2T
1 T. cider vinegar*	2T	¼c	¼c + 2T
¼ t. salt	¾t	1½t	2¼t
⅛ t. pepper	⅜t	¾t	1⅛t
Serving day			
½ cup pecans, chopped			
¼ cup flour			
Olive oil			

* The measurements for the vinegar in the quantity table are correct. The flavor of acidic ingredients is intensified when a recipe is made in large quantity. The recipe has been adjusted to accommodate this.

Original recipe yields

6 servings

Cooking day instructions

For the chicken: Mix olive oil, thyme, garlic, salt, and pepper. Place chicken breasts in freezer bags, then pour olive oil mixture over chicken breasts. Freeze, using freezer bag method.

For the sauce: Melt butter in medium saucepan over low heat. Sauté shallots in butter until tender. Add orange juice and whiskey over medium heat, and continue cooking until liquid is reduced by one half. Add cream. Continue cooking until slightly thickened. Add honey, vinegar, salt, and pepper. Cool. Freeze separately, using freezer bag method.

Serving day instructions

Thaw chicken breasts and cream sauce. Mix chopped pecans and flour together. Dredge chicken breasts in flour mixture. Heat a small amount of olive oil in large skillet. Pan fry chicken breasts until golden brown and cooked through. Heat sauce over low heat until warm; do not boil.

To serve, place chicken on individual serving dishes and pour cream sauce over chicken breasts.

Italian Stuffed Chicken Breasts

Sure to impress when served with Caesar salad and hot bread

	x2	x4	x6
6 boneless, skinless chicken breast halves	12	24	36
Salt and pepper			
Thyme			
Marjoram			
6 oz. mozzarella cheese, cut into 1-ounce sticks	12oz	24oz	36oz
6 thin slices prosciutto ham (see hint below)	12	24	36
12 pcs. oil-packed, sun-dried tomatoes, drained	24	48	72

Serving day

	x2	x4	x6
3–4 T. butter, melted	6–8T	12–16T	18–24T

Tomato cream sauce

2 T. butter or margarine
½–1 T. tomato paste
2 T. flour
¼ t. garlic powder (or 1 clove, finely minced)
Basil (1-2 T. fresh, chopped, or ½ t. dried or to taste)
¼ t. salt
Dash of pepper
1 cup light cream or milk

Original recipe yields

6 servings

Cooking day instructions

Flatten chicken breasts to ⅛-inch thickness (see "Get to Know Your Butcher" on page 16). Sprinkle chicken with salt, pepper, thyme, and marjoram. Wrap each mozzarella stick with 1 slice prosciutto. Place 2 sun-dried tomatoes and 1 wrapped mozzarella stick in center of each chicken breast. Roll chicken breasts around filling. Wrap each chicken breast individually with plastic wrap. Freeze, using freezer bag method.

Serving day instructions

Thaw completely. Unwrap chicken breasts, place close together in baking dish, and baste with butter. Bake at 350 degrees for 35–40 minutes, basting every 15–20 minutes. Do not overbake, as chicken will become tough. Bake just until chicken is white and juices run clear. While chicken is baking, prepare Tomato Cream Sauce. To serve, top chicken breasts with sauce.

For sauce: In a small saucepan, melt butter or margarine. Add tomato paste and blend until smooth. Stir in flour, garlic, basil (if using dried), salt, and pepper. Add cream or milk all at once. Cook and stir over medium heat until thickened and bubbly (if using fresh basil, add now). Cook and stir 1–2 minutes more. Makes approximately 1 cup of sauce.

Hints

Prosciutto is an Italian ham, usually found in the delicatessen area of your grocer. Although it can be pricey, you use very little, as it is sliced so thin.

Leftover sun-dried tomatoes can be used as salad toppers or with fresh pasta dishes.

Lemon Glazed Chicken Breasts

Especially good served with wild rice and mixed greens

	x3	x6	x9
3 boneless, skinless chicken breast halves	9	18	27
½ cup flour	1½c	3c	4½c
½ t. pepper	1½t	1T	4½t
¼ cup butter, melted	¾c	1½c	2¼c
¼ cup honey	¾c	1½c	2¼c
¼ cup lemon juice*	½c	1c	1½c
1 T. soy sauce	3T	¼c + 2T	½c + 1T

* The measurements for the lemon juice in the quantity table are correct. The flavor of acidic ingredients is intensified when a recipe is made in large quantity. The recipe has been adjusted to accommodate this.

Original recipe yields

3 servings

Cooking day instructions

Pound chicken breasts to ½-inch thickness. Mix flour and pepper together. Dredge chicken through flour mixture. Lay breasts flat on cookie sheet, cover with plastic wrap, and flash freeze for one hour.

Mix together butter, honey, lemon juice, and soy sauce. Place in quart-size freezer bag (mixture will be watery). Freeze glaze, using freezer bag method. Place frozen chicken breasts in separate freezer bag and freeze.

Serving day instructions

Allow chicken breasts and glaze to thaw. Place chicken in baking dish, pour glaze over chicken breasts, and bake at 350 degrees for one hour. Glaze will thicken as it cooks.

Orange Teriyaki Chicken

Great on the grill!

	x2	x4	x6
¼ cup soy sauce	½c	1c	1½c
3 T. chopped onion	6T	¾c	1c + 2T
2 cloves garlic, minced	4	8	12
1 T. olive or canola oil	2T	¼c	¼c + 2T
½ t. ground pepper	1t	2t	1T
½ t. ground ginger	1t	2t	1T
½ t. red pepper sauce	1t	2t	1T
1-6 oz. can orange juice concentrate	12oz	24oz	36oz
8 boneless, skinless chicken breasts	16	32	48

Original recipe yields

8 servings

Cooking day instructions

Combine all ingredients except chicken. Place chicken breasts in freezer bag and pour marinade over chicken. Freeze, using freezer bag method.

Serving day instructions

Thaw chicken breasts. Grill 4–6 inches from the heat source for 35–40 minutes.

Oriental Sesame Chicken Strips

You'll love the flavor

	x3	x6	x9
½ cup honey	1½c	3c	4½c
¼ cup orange juice	¾c	1½c	2¼c
2 T. soy sauce	6T	¾c	1c + 2T
1 envelope Good Seasons Oriental Sesame Dressing Mix	3	6	9
4 boneless, skinless chicken breasts (about 1¼ lb.), cut lengthwise into ¾-inch wide strips	12	24	36

Original recipe yields

4 servings

Cooking day instructions

Mix honey, juice, soy sauce, and dressing mix in large bowl until well blended. Place chicken strips in freezer bag. Pour marinade over chicken. Freeze, using freezer bag method.

Serving day instructions

Thaw chicken and thread skewers through each chicken strip. Broil 4 inches from heat or grill over medium coals 8–10 minutes or until cooked through, turning frequently.

Hint

May be served on small wooden skewers as an appetizer or in larger quantities as a main dish.

Pecan Stuffed Chicken Breasts

"Wonderful flavors" describes this gourmet dish

	x3	x6	x9
4 T. (½ stick) butter or margarine	¾c	1½c	2¼c
1 large celery stalk, chopped	3	6	9
1 small onion, minced	3	6	9
1¼ t. salt, divided	3¾ t.	7½ t.	3T + 2 t.
¾ t. pepper, divided	2¼ t.	4½ t.	2T + ¾ t.
2 cups crumbled toast (4 slices bread)	6c	12c	18c
3 oz. pecans, chopped (1 cup)	9oz	18oz	27oz
2 t. parsley flakes	2T	4T	6T
¼ cup water	¾c	1½c	2¼c
4 boned chicken breasts	12	24	36
2 T. lemon juice	6T	¾c	1c + 2T
Melted butter or margarine			

Original recipe yields

4 servings

Cooking day instructions

Melt butter or margarine and cook celery, onion, ½ t. salt, and ¼ t. pepper until tender. Stir in crumbled toast, chopped pecans, parsley flakes, and ¼ cup water. Remove from heat.

Flatten chicken breasts to ⅛-inch thickness (see "Get to Know Your Butcher" on page 16). Place each chicken breast on center of 12-inch square of heavy-duty foil. Brush both sides of breasts with lemon juice and some melted butter or margarine. Sprinkle breasts with ¾ t. salt and ½ t. pepper. Spoon stuffing mixture onto center of each chicken breast, folding chicken breast around stuffing. Bring foil up around breasts and close tightly. Freeze foil bundles, using freezer bag method.

Serving day instructions

Thaw completely, place bundles in pan, and bake at 400 degrees for 20 minutes. Open bundles carefully and brush with drippings in bottom of foil. Bake uncovered for 20 minutes longer or until chicken is fork tender.

Hint

We have found that this recipe makes extra stuffing. You can either increase the number of breasts filled or freeze the extra stuffing in bags to serve as a side dish with this meal or another.

Polynesian Chicken Bundles

A touch of Hawaii

	x3	x6	x9
12 oz. pineapple juice	36oz	72oz	108oz
6 T. soy sauce	1c + 2T	2¼c	3⅓c
4 t. cornstarch	¼c	½c	¾c
2 T. water	¼c + 2T	¾c	1c + 2T
1-15 oz. can fried rice	3	6	9
3 green onions, chopped	9	18	27
1 green pepper, chopped	3	6	9
6 chicken breast halves, pounded flat	18	36	54

Original recipe yields

6 servings

Cooking day instructions

Place juice and soy sauce in saucepan. Mix cornstarch with water and add to saucepan. Heat to boiling; remove from heat.

Heat fried rice in skillet; add green onion and green pepper. Add a little juice from the saucepan to the skillet.

Place one scoop of rice mixture in center of a chicken breast and roll from narrow end, holding together with a toothpick at each end. Continue with each breast until complete. Wrap each individual roll in plastic wrap, and place together in large freezer bag. Freeze sauce in separate freezer bag.

Serving day instructions

Thaw chicken bundles and separate bag of sauce. Preheat oven to 375 degrees. Place rolled chicken breasts in baking dish and pour sauce over them. Bake for 50 minutes, basting with sauce in baking dish after the first 20 minutes. Cover dish for the remaining 30 minutes.

Teriyaki Chicken (or Steak)

Authentic Japanese teriyaki sauce

	x3	x6	x9
2 cups soy sauce*	6c	12c	18c
2 cups sugar	6c	12c	18c
1 cup Mirin (rice cooking wine)**	3c	6c	9c
2 t. fresh ginger, grated	2T	4T	6T
2 t. fresh garlic, minced	2T	4T	6T

* Can be found in much larger quantities in Asian markets.
** Can be found in Asian markets or in some larger grocery stores.

Original recipe yields

Approximately 4½–5 cups of sauce, enough for 7½–8 pounds of meat or poultry

Cooking day instructions

Combine all ingredients and simmer until sugar is dissolved. Cool and store in airtight container (a 1-quart glass jar with lid works great and keeps for several months refrigerated). When you need teriyaki sauce, it's always ready!

For every 1 pound of meat or poultry, place ½ cup sauce in freezer bag together with meat. Freeze, using freezer bag method. Since the sauce contains cooking wine, the marinade will not freeze solid, but the meat will.

Serving day instructions

Thaw meat completely. Grill, bake, or broil to desired doneness. If you use the sauce in the bag to pour over meat, be sure to bring sauce to a full boil for 1–2 minutes before using.

Hint

This sauce can be used for any meat, fish, or poultry. We really like it for flank steak, chicken breasts, sirloin shish-ka-bobs, and shrimp.

Tropical Chicken Ribbons

A tangy surprise for your backyard luau

	x3	x6	x9
¼ cup frozen pineapple-orange-guava juice concentrate, thawed	¾c	1½c	2¼c
2 T. vegetable oil	6T	¾c	1c + 2T
1 T. white wine vinegar	3T	6T	9T
1 clove garlic, pressed	3	6	9
3 sprigs parsley	9	18	27
½ t. ground cumin	1½t	1T	4½t
¼ t. liquid hot pepper sauce	¾t	1½t	2¼t
Salt to taste			
4 boneless, skinless chicken breasts, cut in long strips	12	24	36

Serving day

Fresh pineapple
Onion
Red or green bell pepper

Original recipe yields

4–6 servings

Cooking day instructions

In blender, combine juice concentrate, oil, vinegar, garlic, parsley, cumin, and hot sauce. Blend until smooth; season with salt. Place chicken in freezer bag with marinade. Freeze, using freezer bag method.

Serving day instructions

Thread thawed, marinated chicken onto skewers, weaving chicken strips around chunks of pineapple, onion, and bell pepper. Immediately grill over medium-hot coals on covered grill. May also be broiled in oven for 4–6 minutes on each side.

Turkey Picante Pie

Great-tasting pie with a little zip!

	x2	x4	x6
1 lb. ground turkey	2 lbs	4 lbs	6 lbs
1 large onion, chopped	2	4	6
1 clove garlic, minced	2	4	6
¾ cup picante sauce	1½c	3c	4½c
1 t. ground cumin	2t	4t	2T
½ t. salt	1t	2t	1T
1 large tomato, chopped	2	4	6
1 large zucchini, diced	2	4	6
⅓ cup ripe olives, sliced	⅔c	1⅓c	2c
1½ cups (6 oz.) shredded cheddar and Monterey Jack cheese	12oz	24oz	36oz
2 T. cornstarch	¼c	½c	¾c

Serving day

½ cup shredded cheddar and Monterey Jack cheese

2 pie pastries

Original recipe yields

1 large or 2 small pies

Cooking day instructions

Brown turkey with onion and garlic in large skillet. Stir in picante sauce, cumin, and salt. Simmer for 5 minutes. Remove from heat and stir in tomato, zucchini, olives, 1½ cups cheese, and cornstarch. Freeze, using freezer bag method.

Serving day instructions

Sprinkle ½ cup cheese on pie crust, then spoon mixture over cheese. Top with crust with slits cut in. Bake at 400 degrees for 35 minutes. Let stand for 5 minutes before serving.

Hints

A double batch of this recipe makes 3 medium (9-inch) pies with approximately 3¼ cups of mixture in each pie.

For pie to have pretty glazed look, brush top of pie crust with beaten egg white prior to baking.

Substitution

Ground beef may be used in place of ground turkey.

Beef and Pork

Baked Steak in Tangy Tomato Sauce
Barbecue Spareribs
Beef Chimichangas
Beef Fajitas
Beef Kabobs Dijon
Beef Pita Tacos
Beef Stroganoff
Colorado Style Beef Enchiladas
Continental Beef
Cottage Pie
Dijon Pork Loin Roast
French Steak
Honey Pork Chops
Lemony Flank Steak
London Broil
Meatballs
Molasses-Bourbon Short Ribs
Pinwheel Flank Steak
Pork Chops à la Orange
Rio Rancho Taco Meat
Rocky Mountain Beef Brisket with Barbecue Sauce
Sassy Sloppy Joes
Shish-Ka-Bobs
Shredded Salsa Beef
Sirloin Strips in Wine Sauce
Steak/Chicken Picado
Venezuelan Steak
Very Best Meatloaf
Woodland Park Italian Beef

Baked Steak in Tangy Tomato Sauce

This steak will melt in your mouth

	x3	x6	x9
2 lbs. round or sirloin steak, tenderized	6 lbs	12 lbs	18 lbs
½ t. salt	1½t	1T	4½t
½ t. pepper	1½t	1T	4½t
3 T. shortening	9T	1c + 2T	1½c + 3T
⅓ c. onion, chopped	1c	2c	3c
⅓ c. celery, chopped	1c	2c	3c
1 clove garlic, minced	3	6	9
2 T. brown sugar	6T	¾c	1c + 2T
2 t. yellow mustard	2T	¼c	6T
2 T. Worcestershire sauce	6T	¾c	1c + 2T
2 t. lemon juice	2T	¼c	6T
Dash of Tabasco sauce			
1 cup undiluted tomato soup	3c	6c	9c

Original recipe yields

4 servings

Cooking day instructions

Salt and pepper tenderized steak. Brown meat, onion, celery, and garlic in hot shortening. Add remaining ingredients and cover. Cook for 15–20 minutes. Freeze, using freezer bag method.

Serving day instructions

Thaw completely. Bake covered in 350-degree oven for 1½–2 hours or until tender.

Hint

Ask your butcher to run your steak through a tenderizer at the grocery store when you purchase it. You will have better results with this recipe than if you tenderize the meat yourself.

Barbecue Spareribs

A sweet and sour sauce permeates these ribs

	x2	x4	x6
5 lbs. beef or pork spareribs	10 lbs	20 lbs	30 lbs
1½ cups ketchup	3c	6c	9c
1½ cups water	3c	6c	9c
¼ cup brown sugar	½c	1c	1½c
1 T. soy sauce	2T	¼c	6T
1 T. lemon juice	2T	¼c	6T
¾ cup pineapple juice	1½c	3c	4½c

Original recipe yields

6 servings

Cooking day instructions

Brown spareribs in medium skillet. Combine remaining ingredients in medium saucepan. Bring to boil on stove. Reduce heat and simmer for 10 minutes. Place spareribs in a freezer bag. After sauce has cooled, pour over ribs in bag. Freeze, using freezer bag method.

Serving day instructions

Thaw completely. Place meat and sauce in Crock-Pot and cook on low for 7–8 hours. To bake in oven, place in large baking dish, cover, and bake at 350 degrees for 1½–2 hours.

Beef Chimichangas

Pop out of the freezer and into the oven for a quick meal

	x3	x6	x9
1 t. salt	1T	2T	3T
2 lbs. lean ground beef	6 lbs	12 lbs	18 lbs
2 cloves garlic, crushed	6	12	18
2 t. ground cumin	2T	4T	6T
2 t. oregano, crushed	2T	4T	6T
½ cup canned green chiles, chopped	1½c	3c	4½c
½ cup taco sauce	1½c	3c	4½c
½ cup sour cream	1½c	3c	4½c
¼ cup cider vinegar*	½c	1c	1½c

Serving day

1 cup butter or margarine, melted

9-7 inch flour tortillas

* The measurements for the vinegar in the quantity table are correct. The flavor of acidic ingredients is intensified when a recipe is made in large quantity. The recipe has been adjusted to accommodate this.

Original recipe yields

9 chimichangas

Cooking day instructions

Sprinkle salt in medium skillet. Place over medium heat. Add beef, garlic, and spices. Cook until meat loses pinkness. Stir in remaining ingredients. Remove from heat and cool. Freeze meat mixture, using freezer bag method.

Serving day instructions

In 8-inch skillet, melt butter or margarine. Dip both sides of 1 tortilla into butter; drain off excess. Mound ⅓ cup filling on center of tortilla. Fold tortilla in envelope fashion. Place seam side down in ungreased 11x7 baking dish. Repeat with remaining tortillas and filling.

Preheat oven to 500 degrees. Bake until crispy, about 15 minutes. Sprinkle with cheese and return for a few seconds. Top with cheese, lettuce, tomatoes, avocado, and additional sour cream.

Hint

For a lower-fat version of this recipe, microwave tortillas wrapped in a kitchen towel for 60 seconds to soften. Then fill with mixture, fold in envelope fashion, and brush tops of folded chimis with butter, rather than dipping the tortillas in butter.

Beef Fajitas

Serve with warm tortillas and Spanish rice

	x3	x6	x9
1½ lbs. round steak	4½ lbs	9 lbs	13½ lbs
½ cup fresh lime juice*	1c	1½c	2c
¼ cup tequila	¾c	1½c	2¼c
3–4 cloves garlic, finely minced	9–12	18–24	27–36
1 t. salt	1T	2T	3T
½ t. freshly ground pepper	1½t	1T	4½t

Serving day

1 small onion, thinly sliced into rings

1 T. vegetable oil

1 green pepper, sliced into strips

Warmed flour tortillas

* The measurements for the lime juice in the quantity table are correct. The flavor of acidic ingredients is intensified when a recipe is made in large quantity. The recipe has been adjusted to accommodate this.

Original recipe yields

6 servings

Cooking day instructions

Cut beef into 4 pieces. Place meat in freezer bags with lime juice, tequila, garlic, salt, and pepper. Close bag securely. Freeze, using freezer bag method.

Serving day instructions

Thaw beef and marinade completely. In heavy skillet, sauté onion in oil for 2 minutes. Add green pepper strips and cook for 2 more minutes or until vegetables are crisp-tender.

Drain marinade and discard. Grill beef or stir-fry in heavy skillet over medium-high heat. Carve beef into thin slices. Quickly stir beef and vegetables together in skillet and cook for 1–2 minutes or until heated through.

Fill warmed tortillas with beef and vegetables. Serve with shredded cheese, sour cream, lettuce, tomato, and guacamole as desired.

Substitution

For chicken fajitas, substitute 4 boneless chicken breasts for the beef.

Beef Kabobs Dijon

An amazing variation on traditional kabobs

	x2	x4	x6
5 lbs. sirloin tip roast of beef	10 lbs	20 lbs	30 lbs
Marinade			
2 large cloves garlic, crushed	4	8	12
1 cup vegetable oil	2c	4c	6c
¼ cup soy sauce	½c	1c	1½c
¼ cup Worcestershire sauce	½c	1c	1½c
¼ cup Dijon mustard	½c	1c	1½c
¼ cup fresh lemon juice	½c	1c	1½c
1–2 t. coarsely ground black pepper	2–4t	4–8t	6–12t
Serving day			
2 medium onions			
1 green bell pepper			
1 red bell pepper			
1 yellow bell pepper			
1 lb. mushrooms			
2 pints cherry tomatoes			

Original recipe yields

8 servings

Cooking day instructions

Cut beef into 1½-inch cubes and place in freezer bag. Combine marinade ingredients and pour over meat in bag. Freeze, using freezer bag method.

Serving day instructions

Prepare onions and peppers by cutting into large chunks that can be skewered. Cut off large stems of mushrooms. Assemble skewers, alternating meat with tomatoes, onions, peppers, and mushrooms. Grill over hot coals 3 minutes per side, turning and basting often with marinade.

Beef Pita Tacos

A favorite for families on the run

	x3	x6	x9
1 lb. lean ground beef	3 lbs	6 lbs	9 lbs
1 cup salsa	3c	6c	9c
1-8 oz. can stewed tomatoes	3	6	9

Serving day

4 pita bread, cut in half

Original recipe yields

4 servings (3 cups of meat mixture, or enough for about 8 tacos)

Cooking day instructions

Crumble beef into skillet and cook until no longer pink. Drain fat. Stir in salsa and stewed tomatoes and bring to a boil. Reduce heat and simmer for 6–8 minutes, stirring occasionally, until thickened. Freeze meat mixture, using freezer bag method.

Serving day instructions

Thaw completely. Heat mixture in saucepan until warmed through. Heat pita bread in 350-degree oven for 4–5 minutes. Stuff each pita with ⅓ cup of meat. Serve with shredded lettuce, tomatoes, onion, sour cream, cheese, and avocado as desired.

Beef Stroganoff

Absolutely the best!

	x2	x4	x6
2 lbs. sirloin steak or beef tenderloin	4 lbs	8 lbs	12 lbs
1 lb. fresh mushrooms, sliced	2 lbs	4 lbs	6 lbs
1 cup minced onion	2c	4c	6c
¼ cup butter or margarine	½c	1c	1½c
2-10.5 oz. cans beef bouillon	4	8	12
¼ cup ketchup	½c	1c	1½c
2 small cloves garlic, crushed	4	8	12
2 t. salt	4t	8t	4T
⅓ cup flour	⅔c	1⅓c	2c
2 cups sour cream	4c	8c	12c

Original recipe yields

6–8 servings

Cooking day instructions

Cut meat into bite-size pieces. In skillet, cook and stir mushrooms and onion in butter until onion is tender. Remove mushrooms and onion. In same skillet, brown meat lightly on both sides. Set aside ¾ cup bouillon; add remaining bouillon, ketchup, garlic, and salt to skillet. Stir to mix. Cover and simmer 15 minutes. Blend reserved bouillon and flour; stir into meat mixture. Add mushrooms and onion. Heat to boiling, stirring constantly. Boil 1 minute. Stir in sour cream and heat, but do not allow to boil. Freeze, using freezer bag method.

Serving day instructions

Thaw completely and warm in saucepan until heated through. Do not allow stroganoff to boil when heating. Serve over rice or noodles.

Hints

Doubling this recipe makes 3 meals of stroganoff with 4 cups in each meal.

On serving day, if stroganoff appears too thin, it may be thickened by mixing flour with some sour cream or some of the sauce and adding to mixture while heating.

Colorado Style Beef Enchiladas

A classy layered enchilada dish

	x3	x6	x9
1¼ lb. lean ground beef	3¾ lbs	7½ lbs	11¼ lbs
1 medium onion (about ¾ c.), diced	3	6	9
3–4 T. taco seasoning	9–12T	18–24T	27–36T
½ t. salt, or to taste	1½t	1T	4½t
¼ t. pepper, or to taste	¾t	1½t	2¼t
1 small can mild green chiles, chopped	3	6	9
1-6–8 oz. can green chile salsa (any picante or salsa may be substituted)	3	6	9
¼–⅓ cup water	¾–1c	1½–2c	2¼–3c
Vegetable oil, for quick frying			
12 corn tortillas	36	72	108
1 lb. cheddar or Monterey Jack cheese, grated	3 lbs	6 lbs	9 lbs
Sauce			
1-15 oz. can mild red chile enchilada sauce	3	6	9
1-15 oz. can medium green enchilada sauce (mild green sauce may be substituted)	3	6	9
⅓ cup sour cream	1c	2c	3c
3 T. cream or milk	9 T	1c + 2T	1½c + 3T

Original recipe yields

6–8 servings

Cooking day instructions

Brown meat and diced onion in skillet on medium heat. While meat is browning, prepare sauce (see below). Drain meat and return to pan; add dry taco seasoning, salt, pepper, green chiles, green chile salsa, and ¼–⅓ c. water. Mix well, cover, and simmer on very low heat for 15 minutes. Check meat mixture to see if most of the water has been absorbed. The meat should remain moist. Adjust seasonings at this point (if desired). Cover and keep warm.

▶

For sauce: In medium bowl, combine red and green enchilada sauces, sour cream, and cream or milk. Whisk together until well blended and smooth. (More sour cream or milk may be added if you prefer a less intense sauce.)

In a smaller pan, add 3–4 T. oil and heat over medium heat until hot. Using metal tongs, work quickly and dip each side of a corn tortilla in hot oil (not more than 1–2 seconds per side). Promptly place tortilla on plate lined with paper towels to drain excess oil. Repeat with remaining corn tortillas, adding extra oil to pan as needed.

To assemble: In lined 9x13 baking dish, pour ¾ c. of sauce on bottom of dish to cover. Place a single layer of corn tortillas on sauce. Top with a layer of half the meat mixure, then sprinkle with cheese. Repeat tortilla, meat, and cheese layers. Pour remaining sauce over layers and top with cheese. Cool enchiladas completely. Freeze, using foil and plastic wrap method.

Serving day instructions

Thaw completely. Bake at 350 degrees for 18–20 minutes or until cheese is bubbly and heated through. Serve with shredded lettuce and diced tomatoes, and top with sour cream and/or guacamole.

Continental Beef

Tender meat in a rich sauce, with a great variation

	x2	x4	x6
6 T. butter or margarine	12T	24T	36T
1 cup minced onion	2c	4c	6c
1 lb. fresh mushrooms, sliced (optional)	2 lbs	4 lbs	6 lbs
2½ lbs. beef chuck, cut into cubes (may also substitute other beef suitable for stewing, i.e. beef stew, round steak)	5 lbs	10 lbs	15 lbs
8 oz. can tomato sauce	16oz	32oz	48oz
2 t. Worcestershire sauce	4t	2T + 2t	¼c
1 T. granulated sugar	2T	¼c	¼c + 2T
2 t. paprika	4t	2T + 2t	¼c
2 t. salt	4t	2T + 2t	¼c
⅛ t. pepper	¼t	½t	¾t
2 cloves garlic, minced	4	8	12

Serving day

*1 cup sour cream (optional)

2 cups rice or 16 oz. buttered noodles

Original recipe yields

6–8 servings

Cooking day instructions

Melt 2 T. butter in Dutch oven (or large, deeper stockpot) over low heat. Add onion and mushrooms and brown lightly. Remove from pan. Add more butter (1–2 T.) to pan and melt; add beef in 2 or 3 batches and brown. (You may need to turn heat up slightly to brown meat.) Put beef, mushrooms, and onions back into pan.

Combine tomato sauce, Worcestershire sauce, sugar, paprika, salt, pepper, and garlic. Pour sauce over meat. Cover and cook slowly over low heat for 2½ hours or until meat is tender. Stir occasionally. (Recipe may also be prepared in Crock-Pot for 8–10 hours on low, until beef is tender.) Cool meat mixture. Freeze, using freezer bag method.

Serving day instructions

Thaw meat completely and warm in saucepan until heated through. Do not allow beef mixture to boil when heating. Serve over rice or hot buttered noodles.

   *Variation using sour cream: Just before serving, add sour cream to beef mixture. Stir until smooth and heated through. Do not boil.

Cottage Pie

An all-in-one meat and potatoes dish

	x3	x6	x9
1¼ lb. lean ground beef	3¾ lbs	7½ lbs	11¼ lbs
1 cup onion, chopped	3c	6c	9c
½ t. salt	1½t	1T	4½t
¼ t. pepper	¾t	1½t	2¼t
2 cloves garlic, minced	6	12	18
1-15 oz. can green beans or corn, drained	3	6	9
1-10.5 oz. can tomato soup, undiluted	3	6	9
½ cup mild or medium picante sauce	1½c	3c	4½c
4 cups mashed potatoes	12c	24c	36c
1½ cups cheddar cheese, grated	4½c	9c	13½c

Original recipe yields

One 8x8 baking dish, 4–6 servings (or 2–3 quart baking dish)

Cooking day instructions

Brown ground beef with onion. Add seasonings. Drain off excess grease from ground beef, and spread evenly in a lined casserole dish. Layer green beans or corn on top of beef, followed by tomato soup and picante sauce. Top with mashed potatoes. Sprinkle with cheese. Freeze, using the foil and plastic wrap method.

Serving day instructions

Thaw completely. Bake at 350 degrees for 30–45 minutes or until heated through.

Hints

This recipe is great made up as a casserole or as individual pot pies. Serve with fresh bread or muffins to make a complete meal.

Dijon Pork Loin Roast

It melts in your mouth!

	x3	x6	x9
1 pork loin roast (approx. 5 lbs.), boned, rolled, and tied	3	6	9
Marinade			
½ cup dry white wine	1½c	3c	4½c
¼ cup vegetable oil	¾c	1½c	2¼c
6 T. Dijon mustard	1c + 2T	2¼c	3⅓c
¼ cup mushrooms, chopped	¾c	1½c	2¼c
2 T. soy sauce	6T	¾c	1c + 2T
2 T. fresh lemon juice*	¼c	½c	¾c
2 T. minced onion	6T	¾c	1c + 2T
2 T. butter	6T	¾c	1c + 2T
½ t. celery seed	1½t	1T	4½t
½ t. salt	1½t	1T	4½t
½ t. ground black pepper	1½t	1T	4½t

* The measurements for the lemon juice in the quantity table are correct. The flavor of acidic ingredients is intensified when a recipe is made in large quantity. The recipe has been adjusted to accommodate this.

Original recipe yields

8 servings

Cooking day instructions

In large bowl, mix together all marinade ingredients. Place pork roast in freezer bag. Pour marinade over roast and freeze, using freezer bag method.

Serving day instructions

Allow roast to thaw. Drain and reserve marinade. Roast at 350 degrees for 2½ hours or to an internal temperature of 155–160 degrees. Baste frequently with reserved marinade during last 45 minutes of roasting time.

French Steak

Excellent!!

	x3	x6	x9
2 lbs. round steak	6 lbs	12 lbs	18 lbs
Flour			
Salt and pepper to taste			
2 T. butter	6T	¾c	1c + 2T
1 T. olive oil	3T	6T	9T
2 large onions, thinly sliced	6	12	18
1 clove garlic, minced	3	6	9
1 cup white wine	3c	6c	9c
1 cup beef broth	3c	6c	9c
1 t. Worcestershire sauce	1T	2T	3T
1 t. soy sauce	1T	2T	3T
⅛ t. pepper	⅜t	¾t	1⅛t
1 cup cheddar cheese, grated	3c	6c	9c
½ cup sour cream	1½c	3c	4½c

Original recipe yields

6 servings

Cooking day instructions

Cut steak into serving pieces. Dredge steak with flour seasoned with salt and pepper. Brown on both sides in butter and oil in heavy pan. Remove steak from pan, add onions to pan, and sauté until golden. Stir in garlic, wine, broth, Worcestershire sauce, soy sauce, and pepper, stirring up all the browned bits from bottom of pan. Return steak to pan, cover, and simmer slowly for 1½ hours, until meat is very tender.

Stir in cheese until melted, then stir in sour cream. Heat until sour cream is blended in, but do not boil. Cool completely. Place meat and sauce together in freezer bag. Freeze, using freezer bag method.

Serving day instructions

Thaw meat and sauce completely and place in heavy pan. Heat on stove over low heat until sauce and meat are heated through, but do not boil.

Hint

For a lower-fat entrée, yogurt may be substituted for the sour cream.

Honey Pork Chops

Not your average pork chops

	x3	x6	x9
6 boneless pork chops	18	36	54
½ cup honey	1½c	3c	4½c
¼ cup cider vinegar	¾c	1½c	2¼c
¼ t. ground ginger	¾t	1½t	2¼t
1 clove garlic, minced	3	6	9
2 T. soy sauce	6T	¾c	1c + 2T
Dash of pepper			

Original recipe yields

6 servings

Cooking day instructions

Place all ingredients except pork chops in blender and mix thoroughly. Place pork chops and blended mixture in freezer bag. Seal securely. Freeze, using freezer bag method.

Serving day instructions

Thaw completely. Place pork chops and marinade in baking dish. Bake at 350 degrees for 1¼ hours, turning chops occasionally while baking.

Hint

Pork chops may also be grilled.

Lemony Flank Steak

Serve hot off the grill

	x3	x6	x9
1½ lbs. beef flank steak or boneless beef top sirloin steak	4½ lbs	9 lbs	13½ lbs
1 t. grated lemon peel	1T	2T	3T
⅓ cup lemon juice*	⅔c	1⅓c	2c
2 T. sugar	6T	¾c	1c + 2T
2 T. soy sauce	6T	¾c	1c + 2T
½ t. oregano	1½t	1T	4½t
⅛ t. pepper	⅜t	¾t	1⅛t

* The measurements for the lemon juice in the quantity table are correct. The flavor of acidic ingredients is intensified when a recipe is made in large quantity. The recipe has been adjusted to accommodate this.

Original recipe yields

6 servings

Cooking day instructions

Score meat in 1-inch intervals across steak. Place meat in freezer bags.

Stir together lemon peel, lemon juice, sugar, soy sauce, oregano, and pepper. Pour marinade over meat and close bag. Freeze, using freezer bag method.

Serving day instructions

Thaw, remove steak, and place on uncovered grill over medium coals for 12–14 minutes for medium doneness. Turn once during cooking and brush with marinade halfway through cooking process. (Always boil marinade 2–3 minutes after removing meat and prior to basting grilled steak.)

To serve, meat can be thinly sliced across the grain or served in larger pieces.

London Broil

Great with Bacon-Cheese New Potatoes

	x3	x6	x9
1¼ lbs. top round steak, 1-inch thick	3¾ lbs	7½ lbs	11¼ lbs
⅓ cup cooking oil	1c	2c	3c
1 t. vinegar	1T	2T	3T
1 small clove garlic, minced	3	6	9
Salt and pepper to taste			

Original recipe yields

4–5 servings

Cooking day instructions

Score steak on both sides. Place in freezer bag. Combine oil, vinegar, garlic, salt, and pepper. Pour over meat. Let meat mixture stand at room temperature for 2 hours, then freeze, using freezer bag method.

Serving day instructions

Thaw completely. Remove meat from marinade. Broil steak in oven, 3 inches from heat, for 3–4 minutes per side. Meat may also be grilled. Carve into thin slices across the grain and serve.

Hint

This steak is wonderful served with the following red wine and mushroom sauce.

Red Wine and Mushroom Sauce

1 cup fresh mushrooms, sliced

¼ cup green onion, sliced

2 T. butter or margarine

1 T. cornstarch

½ cup dry red wine

2 T. snipped parsley

1 t. instant beef bouillon granules

¼ t. salt

½ cup water

dash of pepper

Yield: 4 servings

In medium saucepan, cook mushrooms, onion, and butter 4–5 minutes. Stir in cornstarch. Add wine, parsley, bouillon, salt, water, and pepper. Cook and stir until thick and bubbly. Makes 1⅓ cups.

Meatballs

A great thing to have on hand!

	x3	x6	x9
1½ lbs. ground meat	4½ lbs	9 lbs	13½ lbs
¼ cup dry bread crumbs	¾c	1½c	2¼c
⅓ cup onion, chopped	1c	2c	3c
¼ cup milk	¾c	1½c	2¼c
1 egg	3	6	9
1 T. parsley flakes	3T	6T	9T
1 t. salt	1T	2T	3T
⅛ t. pepper	⅜t	¾t	1⅛t
1 T. Worcestershire sauce	3T	6T	9T

Original recipe yields

20 medium meatballs

Cooking day instructions

Combine all ingredients and mix together gently. Shape mixture into balls and arrange on jelly roll pan. Cover meatballs and flash freeze. Remove meatballs from pan and freeze, using freezer bag method.

Serving day instructions

Thaw meatballs completely and place in a 350-degree oven for 30 minutes. Remove from pan and allow to cool.

Hint

Meatballs may be used in a number of ways. They can be served as an appetizer with barbecue sauce, cooked for sandwiches, served with spaghetti sauce, or covered with a cream sauce and placed over pasta or rice.

Barbecue Sauce
(great appetizer!)
1 cup ketchup

1 T. Worcestershire sauce
2 T. brown sugar
2 T. vinegar
¼ t. salt
Dash of pepper

Cream Sauce
(great over meatballs with pasta!)
10.75 oz. can cream of mushroom
soup
8 oz. package cream cheese, softened
½ cup water
½ t. beef bouillon

For both sauces, mix ingredients together and heat until bubbly. Pour over warm meatballs.

Molasses-Bourbon Short Ribs

Awesome for a poolside barbecue

	x2	x4	x6
Molasses-bourbon marinade			
½ cup bourbon	1c	2c	3c
¼ cup molasses	½c	1c	1½c
¼ cup cider vinegar	½c	1c	1½c
½ cup water	1c	2c	3c
1 t. cayenne pepper	2t	4t	2T
½ t. salt	1t	2t	1T
6–7 lbs. beef short ribs, separated into 3–4 slabs	12–14 lbs	24–28 lbs	36–42 lbs
Sauce for barbecuing			
2 T. unsalted butter	4T	8T	12T
3 T. onion, chopped	¼c + 2T	¾c	1c
1 cup ketchup	2c	4c	6c
2 T. molasses	¼c	½c	¾c
2 T. fresh lemon juice	¼c	½c	¾c
2 T. sugar	¼c	½c	¾c
2 T. cider vinegar*	3T	¼c + 2T	¾c
1 T. Worcestershire sauce	2T	¼c	¼c + 2T
1 t. dry mustard	2t	4t	2T
Pepper to taste			

* The measurements for the vinegar in the quantity table are correct. The flavor of acidic ingredients is intensified when a recipe is made in large quantity. The recipe has been adjusted to accommodate this.

Original recipe yields

6–8 servings

Cooking day instructions

For marinade: Combine marinade ingredients. Trim any excess fat from meat. Place ribs in freezer bag; pour marinade over ribs and freeze, using freezer bag method.

For sauce: In medium saucepan, melt butter over low heat, then sauté onion in butter until tender. Add remaining sauce ingredients. Bring to a boil. Reduce heat to simmer, cover, and cook for 15 minutes. Cool completely. Freeze barbecue sauce separately from ribs, using freezer bag method.

Serving day instructions

Thaw completely. Precook by placing ribs and marinade in Crock-Pot and cooking on low for 5–6 hours or until tender. Ribs may also be precooked on grill by wrapping ribs in foil and cooking over medium, indirect heat for approximately 2 hours or until tender. To precook in oven, place ribs in large baking dish with marinade; cover and bake at 350 degrees for 1½–2 hours or until tender.

Once ribs are tender, brush ribs with barbecue sauce and finish by grilling over medium heat for 20 minutes, basting with barbecue sauce frequently.

Pinwheel Flank Steak

Pretty to look at, delicious to taste

	x3	x6	x9
1 beef flank steak, about 1½ lbs.	4½ lbs	9 lbs	13½ lbs
Marinade			
2 cups red burgundy wine	6c	12c	18c
½ cup finely chopped green onions, including tops	1½c	3c	4½c
2 bay leaves, crumbled	6	12	18
1 T. Worcestershire sauce	3T	¼c +2T	½c +1T
1 clove garlic, crushed	3	6	9
1 t. salt	1T	2T	3T
½ t. ground black pepper	1½t	1T	4½t
Filling			
½ lb. bacon	1½ lb	3 lbs	4½ lbs
2 cloves garlic, minced	6	12	18
1 t. salt	1T	2T	3T
½ t. ground black pepper	1½t	1T	4½t
¼ cup minced fresh parsley	¾c	1½c	2¼c
¼ cup finely chopped onion	¾c	1½c	2¼c

Original recipe yields

4 servings

Cooking day instructions

Pound flank steak to ½-inch thickness. Combine all marinade ingredients and mix well. Place flank steak in 9x13 glass or nonaluminum pan, and pour marinade over meat. Marinate for approximately 3–4 hours.

Remove steak from marinade. Fry bacon until almost done but not crisp. Score steak on both sides. Sprinkle steak with garlic, salt, pepper, parsley, and onion. Place bacon lengthwise on steak. Roll up steak, starting with narrow end. Skewer with wooden picks or tie with cotton string at 1½-inch intervals. Place in freezer bag and pour small amount of marinade over rolled steak. Remove as much air as possible from bag. Freeze, using freezer bag method.

Serving day instructions

Partially thaw steak roll. Cut into 1½-inch slices, between wooden picks or strings, and lay flat to finish thawing. Grill over medium-hot coals for 5–7 minutes per side or until desired doneness is achieved, turning once. (Wooden picks or strings are to be left in place through grilling process and removed just prior to eating.) Serve with fresh mango salsa.

Fresh Mango Salsa
A great, versatile salsa for grilled beef, fish, or chicken

1 large ripe mango, peeled, seeded, and diced

⅓ cup finely diced red onion

3 Italian plum tomatoes, seeded and diced

1½ t. finely minced garlic, fresh

1½ T. fresh squeezed lime juice

1 T. finely grated lime zest

1 small jalapeno pepper, cored, seeded, and minced

¼–½ t. salt

2 T. fresh parsley, coarsely chopped

1½ t. sugar (or to taste)

This salsa is best made the day it is served.

In glass bowl, combine all ingredients except parsley. Cover tightly with plastic wrap and chill for at least 30 minutes or up to 4 hours. Just before serving, add parsley and toss. Yields approximately 3 cups.

Hint: If the mango is not as ripe or as sweet as desired, an additional 1–2 t. sugar can be added to the salsa. (Start with smaller amount of sugar and add sparingly until desired sweetness is achieved.)

Pork Chops à la Orange

Oranges and cloves make this a winner

	x3	x6	x9
4 t. flour	¼c	½c	¾c
2 t. seasoning salt	2T	4T	6T
1 t. paprika	1T	2T	3T
¼ t. pepper	¾t	1½t	2¼t
4 pork chops	12	24	36
1 t. cooking oil	1T	2T	3T
½ cup orange juice	1½c	3c	4½c
4 whole cloves	12	24	36
4 thin orange slices	12	24	36
2 T. cold water	6T	¾c	1c + 2T

Original recipe yields

4 servings

Cooking day instructions

Combine flour, seasoning salt, paprika, and pepper. Reserve 1 t. of mixture, and coat pork chops with remaining mixture. Heat oil in skillet, then brown the chops. Add the orange juice and cloves to skillet. Cover and simmer for 45–60 minutes or until tender, turning occasionally.

When tender, add the orange slices and cook 5 minutes longer. Remove the chops and orange slices from skillet. Remove cloves and discard them. Blend reserved flour mixture into 2 T. of cold water and pour it slowly into skillet, stirring constantly. Cook until sauce slightly thickens. Put the pork chops and oranges, along with the cooled sauce, into freezer bag. Freeze, using freezer bag method.

Serving day instructions

Thaw completely. Place pork chops in baking dish and pour sauce over them, placing orange slices around dish. Cover baking dish and place it in a 250-degree oven for approximately 40 minutes or until the sauce is bubbly and the chops are warmed through.

Rio Rancho Taco Meat

Great for tacos, burritos, taco salad, or nachos

	x3	x6	x9
1 medium onion, diced	3	6	9
1½ lbs. ground beef	4½ lbs	9 lbs	13½ lbs
1 cup mild or medium salsa	3c	6c	9c
4–5 T. taco seasoning* or 1 pkg. taco seasoning	¾c (3 pkgs)	1½c (6 pkgs)	2¼c (9 pkgs)
1½ t. brown sugar	4½t	3T	⅓c
1-4 oz. can diced green chiles	3	6	9
1 t. garlic powder or 2 cloves fresh, minced garlic	1T (4)	2T (8)	3T (12)
½ t. salt	1½t	1T	4½t
¼ t. pepper	¾t	1½t	2¼t
¼ t. red pepper, ground or flakes	¾t	1½t	2¼t
¾ cup water	2¼c	4½c	6¾c

* Larger quantities of taco seasoning are available at warehouse clubs such as Sam's and Costco.

Original recipe yields

4–6 servings

Cooking day instructions

Brown onion and ground beef until no longer pink. Drain any excess grease. Add salsa, taco seasoning, brown sugar, green chiles, garlic, salt, pepper, and red pepper. Stir until well mixed. If you like your meat hotter, add more ground red pepper or flakes to taste. Add the water and simmer on low for 30–45 minutes until mixture has thickened and spices have had time to blend. If meat mixture is too thick, add more water and adjust seasonings. Cool. Freeze in meal-size portions, using freezer bag method.

Serving day instructions

Thaw meat mixture or defrost in microwave. Heat through and serve in taco shells or soft, warm tortillas. Top with cheese, lettuce, sour cream, or any of your favorite toppings.

Rocky Mountain Beef Brisket with Barbecue Sauce

Rich and delicious!

	x2	x4	x6
1½ t. salt	1T	2T	3T
1½ t. pepper	1T	2T	3T
2 T. chili powder	¼c	½c	¾c
1 t. crushed bay leaves	2t	4t	2T
2 T. Liquid Smoke	¼c	½c	¾c
4 lbs. beef brisket	8 lbs	16 lbs	24 lbs
Barbecue sauce			
3 T. brown sugar	6T	¾c	1c +2T
1-14 oz. bottle ketchup	2	4	6
½ cup water	1c	2c	3c
2 T. Liquid Smoke	¼c	½c	¾c
Salt and pepper to taste			
4 T. Worcestershire sauce	½c	1c	1½c
1 T. dry mustard	2T	4T	6T
2 t. celery seed	4t	8t	4T
6 T. butter	12T	24T	36T
¼ t. cayenne pepper	½t	1t	1½t

Original recipe yields

6–8 servings

Cooking day instructions

Combine salt, pepper, chili powder, and bay leaves. Rub meat completely with Liquid Smoke. Place meat, fat side up, in large roasting pan. Sprinkle dry seasoning mixture on top. Cover tightly. Bake for 4 hours at 325 degrees. Scrape seasoning and fat off meat, and cut in very thin slices across the grain or shred with 2 forks.

Combine all barbecue sauce ingredients. Bring to a boil, stirring occasionally. Cook for 10 minutes. Pour sauce over meat and mix well to distribute sauce evenly. Freeze in meal-size portions, using freezer bag method.

Serving day instructions

Serve sliced brisket by itself or on fresh rolls.

Hint

We freeze this brisket in packages of 1½ cups each, which makes approximately 6 sandwiches. It is very good and very rich, so a little goes a long way.

Substitution

Chuck steak can be substituted for beef brisket.

Sassy Sloppy Joes

Make a huge batch for the marching band

	x3	x6	x9
½ cup onion, chopped	1½c	3c	4½c
1 T. butter	3T	6T	9T
2 lbs. ground beef	6 lbs	12 lbs	18 lbs
7 oz. ketchup	21oz	42oz	63oz
½ cup water	1½c	3c	4½c
¼ cup celery, chopped	¾c	1½c	2¼c
1 T. lemon juice*	2T	¼c	⅓c
1 T. brown sugar	3T	¼c + 2T	½c + 1T
1½ t. Worcestershire sauce	4½t	3T	¼c + 1t
1½ t. salt	4½t	3T	¼c + 1t
1 t. vinegar	1T	2T	3T
¼ t. dry mustard	¾t	1½t	2¼t

* The measurements for the lemon juice in the quantity table are correct. The flavor of acidic ingredients is intensified when a recipe is made in large quantity. The recipe has been adjusted to accommodate this.

Original recipe yields

15 sandwiches

Cooking day instructions

Sauté onion in butter. Add ground beef; brown lightly. Drain off excess fat. Add remaining ingredients and simmer covered for 30 minutes. Cool mixture and freeze, using freezer bag method.

Serving day instructions

Heat mixture slowly in skillet or saucepan until ready to serve.

Shish-Ka-Bobs

Serve with wild rice and hot bread

	x3	x6	x9
1½ lbs. boneless sirloin	4½ lbs	9 lbs	13½ lbs
½ cup ketchup	1½c	3c	4½c
1 t. salt	1T	2T	3T
2 T. A-1 steak sauce	6T	¾c	1c + 2T
2 T. granulated sugar	6T	¾c	1c + 2T
2 T. cider vinegar	6T	¾c	1c + 2T
2 T. Worcestershire sauce	6T	¾c	1c + 2T
¼ cup water	¾c	1½c	2¼c
2 T. oil	6T	¾c	1c + 2T

Original recipe yields

6 servings

Cooking day instructions

Cut sirloin into cubes and place in freezer bags. Boil marinade ingredients until sugar dissolves. Pour cooled marinade over meat. Seal securely. Freeze, using freezer bag method.

Serving day instructions

Thaw meat completely. Place meat on skewers with onions, mushrooms, green and red peppers, pineapple, and cherry tomatoes. Grill to desired meat temperature.

Hints

Shish-Ka-Bobs can also be cooked under the broiler. Watch closely and rotate skewers to cook meat and vegetables evenly.

When using wooden skewers, soak them in water for 10–15 minutes before skewering meat and vegetables. This will keep the wood from burning.

Substitution

Leaner cuts of beef (ribeye or tenderloin) may be substituted.

Shredded Salsa Beef

A great Crock-Pot recipe—use this filling
for burritos, chalupas, quesadillas, or tacos

	x2	x3
1½–2 lbs. beef roast (chuck or round)	3–4 lbs	4½–6 lbs
1 T. oil	2T	3T
1 onion, chopped	2	3
4 oz. can chopped green chiles	8oz	12oz
1 cup prepared chunky style salsa (mild, medium, or hot)	2c	3c
2 T. brown sugar	¼c	¼c + 2T
1 T. soy sauce	2T	3T
1 clove garlic	2	3
½–1 cup water	1–2c	1½–3c

Serving day

3 T. cilantro, chopped (optional)

Original recipe yields

6–8 servings

Cooking day instructions

Brown meat in skillet in oil on both sides. Place in Crock-Pot. Add remaining ingredients and enough water to barely cover roast. Cover. Cook on low 6–8 hours, depending on Crock-Pot. When beef is tender, remove and shred, using two forks to pull apart. Return meat to Crock-Pot and stir to combine meat and liquid. Meat and sauce can be thickened with flour if you like. Cool. Freeze, using freezer bag method.

Serving day instructions

Thaw beef and reheat slowly in pan. Serve over rice and garnish with cilantro, or use as a filling for tacos, burritos, quesadillas, or chalupas. Serve with cheese, sour cream, lettuce, or your favorite Mexican toppings.

Hint

Beef can also be prepared on stove. Cover tightly and cook slowly over low heat for 3–4 hours, depending on thickness of meat, until fork tender.

Sirloin Strips in Wine Sauce

This entrée has an oriental flare!

	x2	x4	x6
1 small onion, chopped	2	4	6
1 clove garlic, minced	2	4	6
1½ T. butter	3T	6T	12T
Salt and pepper, to taste			
3 lbs. sirloin, cut into strips	6 lbs	12 lbs	18 lbs
15 fresh mushrooms	30	60	90
½ t. basil	1t	2t	1T
½ t. marjoram	1t	2t	1T
1-10.5 oz. can regular-strength beef broth	2	4	6
¼ cup cooking sherry	½c	1c	1½c
1 cup red wine	2c	4c	6c

Serving day

Rice

Cashew nuts

Original recipe yields

8 servings

Cooking day instructions

Brown onion and garlic in butter in skillet. Salt and pepper steak. Add steak to onion mixture and brown. Add mushrooms, basil, marjoram, and beef broth. Cook slowly for 1 hour. Add sherry and cook for ½ hour more. Cool completely. Freeze, using freezer bag method.

Serving day instructions

Thaw completely and reheat in saucepan. Serve over rice with cashews on top.

Hint

On serving day, add steamed broccoli or snow peas to steak mixture if desired.

Steak/Chicken Picado

A salsa-based version of fajitas

	x3	x6	x9
1 lb. flank steak or sirloin	3 lbs	6 lbs	9 lbs
3 T. oil	9T	1c + 2T	1⅔c
1 green pepper, slivered	3	6	9
6 green onions, chopped	18	36	54
½ cup medium or hot salsa	1½c	3c	4½c
¼ cup water	¾c	1½c	2¼c
2 tomatoes, coarsely chopped	6	12	18

Original recipe yields

4–6 servings

Cooking day instructions

Cut steak in half lengthwise, then cut in thin strips across the grain. Brown meat well in oil. Remove meat from pan and add more oil if necessary. Sauté green pepper and onions; drain fat. Return meat to pan and add salsa and water. Cover and simmer 10 minutes. Add tomatoes. Freeze, using freezer bag method.

Serving day instructions

Thaw completely. Cover and simmer on stovetop until heated through. Serve this meal as you would fajitas. Place meat in tortillas with lettuce, sour cream, cheese, rice, or condiments of your choice.

Substitution

The above recipe is very good with chicken substituted in place of the steak.

Venezuelan Steak

Outstanding flavor—this one will catch your fancy

	x3	x6	x9
3 lbs. top round steak or sirloin steak, cut 1½ inches thick	9 lbs	18 lbs	27 lbs
1½ t. unseasoned meat tenderizer (if using round steak, see hint)	4½t	3T	13½t
1 green, red, or yellow bell pepper	3	6	9
4 slices bacon, cut in half	12 slices	24 slices	36 slices
1 medium onion, diced or sliced	3	6	9
¼ cup butter	¾c	1½c	2¼c
½ cup brown sugar	1½c	3c	4½c
⅓ cup vinegar	1c	2c	3c
1 t. salt	1T	2T	3T
2 bay leaves	6	12	18
1-15.5 oz. can tomato sauce	3	6	9

Original recipe yields

6–8 servings

Cooking day instructions

Have your butcher cut a "pocket" in the steak. Sprinkle steak with tenderizer on both sides and inside pocket. (This is very important, especially if using round steak. Sirloin steak is much more tender.) Trim and seed bell pepper, cut into strips, and cook 5 minutes in boiling, salted water; reserve. Cook bacon until limp; drain off drippings and reserve. Stuff steak with bacon, onions, and peppers. Skewer pocket shut using wooden toothpicks inserted at an angle.

Sauté steak in reserved bacon drippings (or if you prefer, use vegetable oil) until both sides are evenly browned. Allow steak to cool.

In another pan, melt butter; add brown sugar and stir until it bubbles. Add vinegar, salt, bay leaves, and tomato sauce and mix well. Cool sauce.

Wrap steak in plastic wrap and seal. Freeze, using freezer bag method. Freeze sauce separately in smaller bag, using freezer bag method. (Label clearly, keeping steak and sauce together in freezer.)

▶

Serving day instructions

Thaw steak and sauce completely. Preheat oven to 325 degrees. Place steak in 9x13 baking dish and pour sauce over meat. Bake 1¾–2 hours or until meat is tender. Slice across grain to serve.

Hints

As a courtesy to their customers, most supermarket meat departments cut pockets or tenderize meats upon request. Be sure to give them time to do so.

Instead of using unseasoned meat tenderizer (when using round steak or a less lean cut), have the butcher tenderize the meat for you. Don't worry that the meat appears to have small holes in it; the stuffing will stay intact just fine.

Very Best Meatloaf

*This is **not** your mom's meatloaf!*

	x3	x6	x9
1 T. oil	3T	6T	9T
1 small onion, chopped	3	6	9
2 cloves of garlic, minced	6	12	18
1 t. thyme	1T	2T	3T
⅓ cup milk	1c	2c	3c
1 egg	3	6	9
¼ cup ketchup	¾c	1½c	2 ¼c
½ cup bread crumbs	1½c	3c	4½c
1¼ t. salt	3¾t	7½t	3T + 2t
½ t. pepper	1½t	1T	4½t
½ lb. ground beef	1½ lbs	3 lbs	4½ lbs
½ lb. ground pork	1½ lbs	3 lbs	4½ lbs
½ lb. ground veal	1½ lbs	3 lbs	4½ lbs

Original recipe yields

2 loaves

Cooking day instructions

Heat oil and cook onion until soft, about 5 minutes. Add garlic and thyme and cook 1 minute more; set aside. Combine milk, egg, and ketchup. Stir in bread crumbs, salt, and pepper. Crumble in meats and add onion mixture. Stir until well combined. Freeze meat into loaves, using the foil and plastic wrap method.

Serving day instructions

On serving day, thaw loaf and place in baking dish. Bake at 350 degrees for 1½ hours. If desired, mix ½c. ketchup and 2T. brown sugar to create sauce and pour over meatloaf for last ½ hour of baking time.

Hint

Ground veal can usually be found prepackaged in 1-pound rolls in the meat department. Sometimes it is prefrozen, which will not affect quality or taste. Defrost the veal slightly and continue to mix with ingredients as directed.

Substitution

Ground turkey can be substituted for either the pork or veal.

Woodland Park Italian Beef

Wonderful served on French baguettes

	x2	x4	x6
2–3 lb. roast (rump, chuck, or pot)	4–6 lbs	8–12 lbs	12–18 lbs
2 large onions, sliced	4	8	12
1–2 green peppers, diced or sliced	2–3	5–6	7–9
2-16 oz. jars Pepperoncini peppers with juice, sliced (or cut up if whole)	4	8	12
½–1 cup water	1–2c	2–4c	3–6c
1 t. fresh ground pepper, sprinkled on top of roast	2t	4t	2T

Serving day

French rolls, sliced

Provolone cheese slices

Original recipe yields

8–10 servings

Cooking day instructions

Cut roast into approximately 4x4 chunks. Put meat into large roasting pan with onion and green pepper. Sprinkle with fresh ground pepper. Pour Pepperoncini peppers (with juice) and water over meat mixture. Bake at 275 degrees for 5 hours. When meat is done and fork tender, remove beef and shred with 2 forks. Turn oven temperature to warm (or 200 degrees). Return beef into pan, mix with pan juices, and let sit in oven for 1 hour. Cool. Freeze in meal-size portions, using freezer bag method.

Serving day instructions

Thaw meat and gently reheat. Place rolls open on baking sheet. Place a slice of provolone cheese on each half of roll. Place under broiler until melted. Top with beef and serve.

Hint

Pepperoncini peppers can be found in the condiment aisle, next to the pickles.

Pasta and More

Barbecue Chicken Pizza
Chicken Alfredo Pizza
Italian Sausage and Green Pepper Cannoli
Manicotti
No-Fail Egg Noodles
No-Rise Pizza Dough
Penne with Chicken, Broccoli, and Cheese
Quick Mix Pizza Dough
Spaghetti Carbonara
Spaghetti Sauce
Spinach Lasagna

Barbecue Chicken Pizza

Make two—it disappears quickly

	x2	x4	x6
3 boneless, skinless chicken breast halves	6	12	18
1⅓ cups purchased barbecue sauce, divided	2⅔c	5⅓c	8c
1 pizza crust	2	4	6
6 oz. provolone cheese, grated	12oz	24oz	36oz
6 oz. Gouda cheese, grated	12oz	24oz	36oz
½ medium red onion, peeled and thickly sliced	1	2	3

Serving day

¼ cup fresh cilantro, chopped

Original recipe yields

One large or two small pizzas

Cooking day instructions

Marinate chicken in ⅔ cup barbecue sauce for 4 hours or up to overnight. Place chicken and marinade in small baking dish. Bake at 350 degrees 30 minutes or until chicken is tender and no longer pink. Remove from oven. Roll out pizza dough to form crust; you may want to use a round cardboard covered with plastic wrap for this step. (Round cardboards may be purchased at any craft store in the baking section.)

Spread remaining ⅔ cup barbecue sauce over crust. Sprinkle cheeses evenly over crust, leaving ½-inch border. Shred chicken and arrange over cheese, topping with onion. Freeze, covering pizza and cardboard with plastic wrap, followed by heavy-duty foil.

Serving day instructions

Preheat oven to 450 degrees. Place frozen pizza on preheated pizza stone and bake 10–12 minutes. Sprinkle with cilantro and serve.

Chicken Alfredo Pizza

An elegant pizza, perfect for entertaining

	x2	x4	x6
Alfredo sauce			
¼ cup butter	½c	1c	1½c
scant 1 cup heavy cream	2c	4c	6c
⅔ cup freshly grated Parmesan cheese	1⅓c	2⅔c	4c
Salt and pepper, to taste			
Pizza			
1 pizza crust	2	4	6
10 large fresh spinach leaves, rinsed and dried	20	40	60
6 green onions, sliced diagonally, including tops	12	24	36
2 boneless, skinless chicken breast halves, cooked and shredded	4	8	12
½ lb. bacon, cut into ½-inch pieces, cooked until crisp	1 lb	2 lbs	3 lbs
1 cup grated mozzarella cheese	2c	4c	6c
1 cup grated Swiss cheese	2c	4c	6c

Original recipe yields

One large or two small pizzas

Cooking day instructions

For sauce: Melt butter in large saucepan or skillet. Add cream and bring to a boil. Simmer for 5 minutes, stirring continuously. Add Parmesan cheese and salt and pepper to taste. Turn off heat under pan.

For pizza: Roll out pizza dough to form crust. (See previous recipe for information on using a round cardboard for this step.) Spread alfredo sauce evenly over pizza crust. Arrange spinach leaves over sauce. Add green onions, shredded chicken, and bacon. Sprinkle cheeses over top. Freeze, covering pizza and cardboard with plastic wrap, followed by heavy-duty foil.

Serving day instructions

Place frozen pizza on pizza stone or baking pan and thaw. Preheat oven to 450 degrees. Bake 15 minutes or until bubbly.

Italian Sausage and Green Pepper Cannoli

Great for your next Super Bowl party

	x3	x6	x9
4 lbs. Italian link sausage, cut into 3–4 inch links	12 lbs	24 lbs	36 lbs
2 large bell peppers, red or green	6	12	18
¼ cup olive oil	¾c	1½c	2¼c
½ t. salt	1½t	1T	4½t
2 cloves garlic, minced	6	12	18

Dough

	x3	x6	x9
1 t. salt	1T	2T	3T
5 cups flour	15c	30c	45c
1½ cup water	4½c	9c	13½c
2 t. active dried yeast	2T	¼c	6T
1 t. sugar	1T	2T	3T
2 T. olive oil	¼c + 2T	¾c	1c + 2T

Original recipe yields

12 small cannolis

Cooking day instructions

Cook sausage in 375-degree oven for 25 minutes. Let cool.

Clean and quarter peppers. Combine oil, salt, garlic, and peppers in large baking dish. Roast uncovered in 400-degree oven for 25–30 minutes until soft. Let cool.

For dough: Sift salt and flour in large bowl. In small bowl, combine ½ cup water, yeast, and sugar. Let stand until foamy. Add yeast mixture, olive oil, and remaining water to flour. Knead until smooth. Let dough rest about 30–45 minutes, until it doubles in size. Pinch about ¼ cup of dough and roll into 2-inch balls. Let rest 20 minutes.

Flatten dough with palm of hand. Place 1–2 pepper strips across dough. Place cooked sausage link on top of peppers. Fold ends over sausage, leaving sides open. Place folded seam down on parchment paper–covered cookie sheet and flash freeze for 30 minutes. Freeze, using freezer bag method.

Serving day instructions

Thaw and let rise 25–30 minutes, until dough doubles in size. Bake at 400 degrees for 25 minutes. Remove from oven and serve with your favorite marinara sauce.

Hint

Cannolis may be filled with any of your favorite pizza toppings!

Manicotti

A great meatless entree

	x3	x6	x9
8–10 manicotti shells	30	60	90
1 lb. (2 cups) ricotta cheese	6c	12c	18c
1 T. parsley	3T	6T	9T
1 egg, beaten	3	6	9
½ t. salt	1½t	1T	4½t
¼ t. pepper	¾t	1½t	2¼t
½ cup Parmesan cheese	1½c	3c	4½c
½ cup mozzarella cheese	1½c	3c	4½c

Serving day

Marinara or spaghetti sauce

Parmesan cheese

Original recipe yields

8–10 servings

Cooking day instructions

Cook manicotti shells according to package directions (see hint below). Mix all ingredients together and fill manicotti shells. Wrap shells in plastic wrap (2 or 3 together or see hint below). Freeze, using freezer bag method.

Serving day instructions

Pour sauce over bottom of ungreased baking dish. Lay stuffed manicotti noodles on top of sauce and top with leftover sauce. Then top with Parmesan cheese and bake at 425 degrees for 30–35 minutes.

Hints

Slightly undercook manicotti shells when preparing for freezer. This will make it easier to fill them and prevent overcooking when reheated.

A pastry bag (or plastic bag with a corner cut off) is a great tool for filling manicotti shells quickly.

Most manicotti shells are stored in individual, lightweight plastic trays. After stuffing the shells, place them back into trays. Wrap thoroughly with plastic wrap, then place trays in freezer bag.

No-Fail Egg Noodles

Just plain good eating!

	x2
1 egg	2
3 egg yolks	6
3 T. cold water	6T
1 t. salt	2t
2 cups flour	4c

Serving day

Butter

Chopped parsley (optional)

Original recipe yields

5½ cups

Cooking day instructions

In mixing bowl, beat egg and yolks until light and fluffy (you might want to save the leftover egg whites to make Frozen Chocolate Meringue Torte). Add water and salt; mix well. Stir in flour (see hint below). Turn onto a floured surface; knead until smooth. (Kneading can be done in an electric mixer using a dough hook. Don't overprocess.)

Divide dough into thirds. Roll out each portion to ⅛-inch thickness. Cut noodles using a knife or pastry cutter wheel. (A clean plastic ruler can also be used as a guide.) Cut noodles to desired width and length.

Uncooked, cut noodles may be stored (tightly wrapped) in refrigerator for 2–3 days or frozen into side-dish serving portions. Noodles can be frozen for 1–2 months. To freeze, double wrap noodles securely with plastic wrap, and place inside freezer bag. Freeze, using freezer bag method.

Serving day instructions

Thaw frozen noodles in refrigerator. Drop noodles into boiling, salted water or chicken broth for 7–9 minutes or until tender. Drain, dot with butter, season according to taste, and sprinkle with parsley, if desired. Toss gently and serve immediately.

Hint

Create different flavors of noodles. Fresh or dried herbs can be added to the flour before mixing. Try using fresh or dried basil, oregano, thyme, dill, red pepper, or coarse ground black pepper. The possibilities are endless!

Substitutions

For an Italian twist, substitute garlic butter, freshly grated Parmesan cheese, and fresh basil for butter and parsley.

Dress up any broth-based soup (chicken broth, vegetable, minestrone, and so on) by dropping uncooked noodles into boiling soup.

No-Rise Pizza Dough

For when you're in a hurry

2 cups very warm water (not hot)
2 packages yeast
3 T. flour
5 cups flour (can use all-white flour; ½ wheat +½ white; or all-wheat, if freshly ground)
3 T. sugar
1 T. salt
Cornmeal (for dusting bottom of pizza)
1 T. oil

Original recipe yields

2 large pizza crusts (medium thickness) or 1 deep-dish and 1 large crust (medium thickness)

Cooking day instructions

This recipe works best by preparing single batches.

In large bowl, combine warm water, yeast, and 2 T. flour. Sprinkle 1 T. flour on top of mixture. Wait until flour is totally absorbed, then add remaining ingredients.

Knead the dough:

- By hand: 7–10 minutes or until very smooth and elastic, not stiff.
- By electric (stand) mixer: Knead, using dough hook, until dough begins to clean sides of mixing bowl (6–12 minutes, depending on your mixer). Do not allow dough to get too stiff.

Divide dough in two. Roll out on cornmeal-dusted pizza paddle, pizza stone, or counter. Brush crust lightly with canola or olive oil and prick with fork every ½–1 inch. Prebake 5–8 minutes in preheated 500-degree oven. Remove crust from oven and cool.

- To freeze unfilled pizza dough shells: Stack pizza shells using plastic wrap or waxed paper between each shell or freeze individually.
- To freeze topped pizzas: Top with desired ingredients. Freeze, using plastic wrap and foil method.

Serving day instructions

Thaw slightly. Preheat oven to 450 degrees. If unfilled, add your favorite toppings. Bake pizza for 15–20 minutes or until crust is nicely browned and cheese is melted.

Penne with Chicken, Broccoli, and Cheese

This recipe should not be frozen.
Eat immediately after preparing—it is delicious!

1 cup broccoli florets, divided into tiny sprigs
¼ cup butter
2 skinless chicken breast halves, cut into thin strips
2 garlic cloves, crushed
Salt and black pepper, to taste
3½ cups penne pasta
½ cup dry white wine
1 cup heavy cream
3½ oz. Gorgonzola cheese, rind removed and diced small
Parmesan cheese, freshly grated

Original recipe yields

4 servings

Cooking and serving day instructions

Plunge broccoli in a saucepan of boiling salted water. Return to a boil and boil for 2 minutes, then drain in colander under cold running water. Shake to remove surplus water and set aside to drain completely.

Melt butter in large skillet or saucepan. Add chicken and garlic, with salt and pepper to taste; stir well. Fry over medium heat for 3 minutes or until chicken becomes white. Meanwhile, begin cooking pasta according to package instructions.

Pour wine and cream over chicken mixture in pan. Stir to mix, then simmer, stirring occasionally, for about 5 minutes, until sauce has reduced and thickened. Increase heat, add broccoli, and toss to heat through. Taste for seasoning and adjust if necessary.

Drain pasta and add it to sauce. Add Gorgonzola and toss well. Top with Parmesan cheese and serve immediately.

Quick Mix Pizza Dough

Works every time

	x2	x4	x6
1 cup water	2c	4c	6c
2 T. olive oil	¼c	½c	¾c
3–3½ cups flour	6–7c	12–14c	18–21c
1 pkg. active dry yeast	2	4	6
1 t. sugar	2t	4t	2T
½ t. salt	1t	2t	1T

Original recipe yields

2 medium or large crusts, depending on thickness

Cooking day instructions

Heat water and olive oil to 120 degrees. In bowl, combine 1½ cups flour with yeast, sugar, and salt. Add warm water and mix with electric mixer for 3 minutes. Stir in 1½ cups additional flour by hand to form a soft dough. Knead on a floured surface for 10 minutes, adding rest of flour as needed. Dough should be smooth and elastic but not sticky. Shape into ball and place in greased bowl. Cover with a damp cloth. Let rise in a warm place about 45 minutes or until doubled in size. Punch down dough and divide in half. Wrap each half in plastic wrap and freeze, using freezer bag method.

Serving day instructions

Thaw completely. Preheat oven to 450 degrees. Roll out pizza dough directly onto pizza pan or baking stone. Prick crust with fork, then parbake in oven for 10–15 minutes or until lightly browned. Remove from oven, add toppings, and return to oven to continue baking for 10–15 more minutes until done.

Spaghetti Carbonara

This dish is best served the day it's prepared, but it is too unbelievably delicious not to include in this book!

1 lb. dry spaghetti
1 lb. cooked bacon, crumbled
1 cup frozen petite peas
2½ cups heavy cream
1 cup fresh Parmesan cheese, grated
1 T. fresh Italian parsley, chopped
Freshly ground black pepper

Original recipe yields

6 servings

Cooking and serving day instructions

Bring large pot of salted water to a boil. Add pasta and cook until al dente, about 8–9 minutes. Drain and set pasta aside.

In large frying pan over medium-high heat, heat bacon pieces until they begin to sizzle. Add peas and cream. Bring sauce to a boil, reduce heat slightly, and boil gently for about 8 minutes. Sprinkle in Parmesan cheese, stirring continuously until blended and sauce is slightly thickened.

Mix pasta and sauce together in large serving bowl. Garnish with chopped parsley and black pepper to taste.

Spaghetti Sauce

A Midwest family favorite

	x2	x4	x6
2 cups onion, chopped	4c	8c	12c
4 cloves garlic, minced	8	16	24
¾ cup oil	1½c	3c	4½c
23 cups tomato, chopped	46c	92c	138c
2 green peppers, chopped	4	8	12
4-12 oz. cans tomato paste	8	16	24
2 T. salt	¼c	½c	¾c
1 T. pepper	2T	¼c	6T
1½ t. oregano	1T	2T	3T
4 bay leaves	8	16	24

Original recipe yields

6 quarts plus one pint

Cooking day instructions

In stockpot, cook onion and garlic in oil until tender but not brown. Puree chopped tomatoes and green peppers in blender. Add tomatoes, peppers and rest of ingredients to sauteed onion and garlic. Bring to simmer. Cook one hour uncovered, stirring frequently. Remove bay leaves. Freeze in freezer bags or quart jars, leaving at least 1 inch head space for expansion. To can the spaghetti sauce, fill hot jars and process in water bath for 30 minutes (add 10 minutes for high altitude).

Serving day instructions

If frozen, thaw completely, then use as desired.

Hint

If freezing the spaghetti sauce, meat may be browned and added to recipe. *Do not* add meat if sauce is to be canned.

Substitutions

Italian sausage or ground beef may be added *only* if you are freezing the sauce.

If you like a slightly "sweeter" sauce, corn syrup or brown sugar can be added. Add according to your taste preference.

Spinach Lasagna

A tasty vegetarian dish

	x3	x6	x9
2 T. olive oil, divided	6T	¾c	1c + 2T
1 medium onion, finely chopped	3	6	9
½ t. crushed red pepper flakes	1½t	1T	4½t
3 cloves garlic, minced	9	18	27
½ lb. fresh mushrooms, sliced	1½ lbs	3 lbs	4½ lbs
1-8 oz. can tomato sauce	3	6	9
1-28 oz. can whole tomatoes, including liquid	3	6	9
1-6 oz. can tomato paste	3	6	9
1 t. salt	1T	2T	3T
1 t. oregano	1T	2T	3T
½ t. basil	1½t	1T	4½t
½ cup red wine	1½c	3c	4½c
1 egg	3	6	9
1-10 oz. package frozen chopped spinach, thawed and well drained	3	6	9
1 cup ricotta cheese	3c	6c	9c
½ cup freshly grated Parmesan cheese	1½c	3c	4½c
8 oz. lasagna noodles, cooked and drained	24oz	48oz	72oz
1 lb. mozzarella cheese, grated	3 lbs	6 lbs	9 lbs

Original recipe yields

6–8 servings

Cooking day instructions

In large sauté pan, heat 1 tablespoon oil. Sauté onion, red pepper flakes, and garlic.

Add mushrooms and sauté gently. Blend in tomato sauce, canned tomatoes with liquid, tomato paste, salt, oregano, basil, and wine. Simmer about 15 minutes, breaking tomatoes into small pieces as mixture cooks.

In medium bowl, mix egg with spinach, ricotta cheese, Parmesan cheese, and remaining 1 tablespoon oil.

Line 9x13 baking dish. To assemble, pour half of sauce into baking dish. Cover with half of lasagna noodles. Spread entire spinach mixture over lasagna noodles. Sprinkle with half of mozzarella cheese. Repeat, layering with remaining lasagna, then sauce, and ending with remainder of mozzarella cheese. Cool completely. Freeze, using foil and plastic wrap method.

Serving day instructions

Remove lasagna from freezer and thaw slightly. Remove foil and plastic wrap from still-frozen lasagna, and return lasagna to original baking dish. Finish thawing. Bake at 350 degrees for 1 hour.

Hint

An extra time-saving tip: prepared spaghetti sauce may be substituted for the tomato sauce recipe above.

Now for Dessert

Almond Cookies
Aunt Clara's Dutch Apple Pie
Cashew Fudge Tarts
Chocolate Butter Cookies
Chocolate Mint Snaps
Chocolate Orange Mousse
Coconut Buttons
Creamy Lemon Cheesecake
Easy Pie Crust
English Toffee
Frozen Chocolate Meringue Torte
Frozen Orange Dream Pie
Frozen Pumpkin Dessert
Heartland Brownies
Homemade Hot Fudge Sauce
Incredible Chocolate Fondue
Light and Flaky Pie Crust
Mom's Blueberry Pie
Oatmeal Chocolate Chip Cookies
Peanut Butter Bars
Peanut Butter Monster Cookies
Sugar Cookies

Almond Cookies

Make plenty!!

	x2	x4	x6
1 cup sugar	2c	4c	6c
1 cup powdered sugar	2c	4c	6c
1 cup butter or margarine	2c	4c	6c
1 cup oil	2c	4c	6c
1 t. almond extract	2t	4t	2T
2 eggs	4	8	12
3½ cups flour	7c	14c	21c
1 cup whole wheat flour	2c	4c	6c
1 t. soda	2t	4t	2T
1 t. salt	2t	4t	2T
1 t. cream of tartar	2t	4t	2T
2 cups chopped almonds	4c	8c	12c
6 oz. English toffee bits (Skor brand)	12oz	24oz	36oz

Original recipe yields

8–10 dozen cookies

Cooking day instructions

Blend sugar, powdered sugar, butter, and oil until well mixed. Add almond extract and eggs and mix well. Lightly spoon and blend in flours, soda, salt, and cream of tartar at low speed. By hand, stir in almonds and toffee bits. Shape into balls and roll in sugar. Crisscross balls with fork dipped in sugar. Bake at 350 degrees on ungreased cookie sheets for 12–18 minutes. Cool on cookie sheets for 1 minute, then remove. Freeze, using instructions for baked goods.

Hints

For fresh-baked cookies, cookie dough balls may be flash frozen on cooking day, then thawed and baked on serving day.

English toffee bits are usually located in the baking section of your grocery store (near the chocolate chips).

Aunt Clara's Dutch Apple Pie

A family favorite handed down through generations

	x3	x6	x9
1 unbaked 9-inch pie shell	3	6	9
Filling			
½ cup sugar (adjust as needed for tartness of apples)	1½c	3c	4½c
1 t. cinnamon	1T	2T	3T
6–8 baking apples, peeled, cored, and sliced	18–24	36–48	54–72
Topping			
¾ cup flour	2¼c	4½c	6¾c
½ cup sugar	1½c	3c	4½c
⅓ cup margarine	1c	2c	3c

Original recipe yields

One 9-inch pie

Cooking day instructions

Place unbaked pie shell in 9-inch disposable pie plate. For apple filling, mix sugar, cinnamon, and apples. Stir until well mixed. Place apple mixture in unbaked pie shell. Make Dutch apple topping by mixing flour, sugar, and margarine with a fork until crumbly. Sprinkle over top of apples. Double wrap pie pan with plastic wrap and freeze.

Serving day instructions

Pie may be baked while still frozen. Bake at 425 degrees for 15 minutes, then at 350 degrees for 45 minutes, until apples are tender and crust lightly browned.

Cashew Fudge Tarts

A classy holiday cookie

Pastry

3 cups flour

6 T. sugar

1½ cups butter or margarine, softened

Filling

1-14 oz. can sweetened condensed milk

1 egg

1 t. instant coffee granules

1 T. hot water

6 oz. semisweet chocolate chips, melted

2 T. flour

1 t. vanilla

¼ t. baking powder

1½ cups lightly salted dry-roasted cashews, coarsely chopped and divided

Original recipe yields

About 5½ dozen tarts

Cooking day instructions

For pastry, combine flour and sugar in medium bowl. Using a pastry blender, cut in butter until mixture resembles coarse meal. Knead in bowl until a soft dough forms. Shape dough into balls, using ½ T. of dough for each. Press balls of dough into bottoms and up sides of greased miniature muffin pans.

Preheat oven to 350 degrees. For filling, whisk milk and egg together in medium bowl. In small bowl, combine coffee and water; stir until coffee is dissolved. Add coffee mixture and next four ingredients to milk mixture; beat with electric mixer until smooth. Stir in 1 cup cashews.

Spoon about 1 T. filling into each pastry. Sprinkle remaining cashews evenly over filling. Bake 25–30 minutes or just until set in center. Cool in pans 10 minutes. Transfer to wire rack to cool completely. Freeze, using instructions for baked goods.

Chocolate Butter Cookies

These small cookies melt in your mouth

	x2	x4	x6
½ cup sugar	1c	2c	3c
¾ cup butter, softened	1½c	3c	4½c
1 egg yolk	2	4	6
1 t. almond extract	2t	4t	2T
1½ cups flour	3c	6c	9c
¼ cup unsweetened cocoa	½c	1c	1½c

Original recipe yields

3–4 dozen cookies

Cooking day instructions

In large bowl, combine sugar, butter, egg yolk, and almond extract. Beat until light and fluffy, approximately 2–3 minutes. Gradually add flour and cocoa until well mixed. Shape (see hint below) and place 1 inch apart on cookie sheet. Bake at 375 degrees on ungreased cookie sheets for 7–9 minutes or until set. Cool completely. Freeze, using instructions for baked goods.

Hint

Cookie dough may be shaped into balls or squares, or dough may be put in a cookie press to form desired shapes.

Chocolate Mint Snaps

A tried and true combination of mint and chocolate

	x3	x6	x9
6 oz. semisweet chocolate chips	18oz	36oz	54oz
1¾ cups flour	5¼c	10½c	15¾c
2 t. baking soda	2T	4T	6T
1 t. cinnamon	1T	2T	3T
¼ t. salt	¾t	1½t	2¼t
⅔ cup shortening	2c	4c	6c
½ cup sugar	1½c	3c	4½c
1 egg	3	6	9
¼ cup light corn syrup	¾c	1½c	2¼c
¼ t. mint extract	¾t	1½t	2¼t

Original recipe yields

3 dozen cookies

Cooking day instructions

Melt chocolate in double boiler. Combine flour, soda, cinnamon, and salt and set aside. Combine shortening, sugar, and egg. Add syrup, extract, and melted chocolate. Gradually blend in the flour mixture. Shape into balls and roll in sugar. Bake at 350 degrees on ungreased cookie sheets for 10–12 minutes. Freeze, using instructions for baked goods.

Hint

For fresh-baked cookies, dough balls may be flash frozen on cooking day, then thawed and baked on serving day.

Chocolate Orange Mousse

Best prepared fresh

6-1 oz. squares semisweet chocolate

1 t. grated orange rind

¼ cup brown sugar, packed

2 egg yolks

2 eggs

1 T. triple sec or orange juice

1 cup whipping cream

Whipped cream

Mandarin oranges

Original recipe yields

5–6 servings

Serving day instructions

Melt chocolate over hot water in top of double boiler, or melt in microwave oven. Cool. Combine orange rind, brown sugar, egg yolks, and eggs in container of electric blender. Blend until light and foamy. Add chocolate and triple sec, blending well. Beat whipping cream and fold into mixture. Pour into dessert dishes. Chill until set. Garnish with whipped cream and mandarin orange slices.

Coconut Buttons

A cute and sassy cookie

	x2	x4
1 cup butter, softened	2c	4c
½ cup sugar	1c	2c
2 T. milk	¼c	½c
1 t. coconut extract (optional)	2t	4t
¾ t. baking powder	1½t	1T
½ t. salt	1t	2t
2⅔ cups flour	5⅓c	10⅔c
1½ cups flaked coconut	3c	6c
4-1oz. squares semisweet chocolate	8oz	16oz
1 T. shortening	2T	4T

Original recipe yields

60–80 buttons

Cooking day instructions

On medium-high speed, beat butter, sugar, milk, extract, baking powder, and salt until light and fluffy. With a spoon, stir in flour and coconut (will be crumbly). With your hands, squeeze the dough together and divide into 4 equal pieces. Shape each into a 10x1-inch log. Wrap each log in plastic wrap and slide onto a small cookie sheet. Refrigerate for 1 hour.

Cut log into ½-inch slices. Heat oven to 325 degrees. Place slices 1 inch apart on ungreased cookie sheets. Make four holes in each cookie to resemble a button. Place on 2 oven racks. Bake 20–25 minutes or until lightly golden, rotating sheets.

When cool, melt chocolate with shortening and dip bottom of each cookie into chocolate. Scrape excess chocolate from the bottom of each cookie, leaving a thin layer. Freeze, using instructions for baked goods.

Hint

Freeze baked cookies in airtight container with sheet of waxed paper between layers.

Creamy Lemon Cheesecake

So good that it's worth every minute of preparation!

	x2	x4	x6
Crust			
2¼ cups graham cracker crumbs	4½c	9c	13½c
¼ cup sugar	½c	1c	1½c
6 T. butter, melted	¾c	1½c	2¼c
Filling			
24 oz. cream cheese, softened	48oz	96oz	144oz
3 eggs	6	12	18
1⅓ cups sugar	2⅔c	5⅓c	8c
3 T. lemon juice	6T	¾c	1c + 2T
2 t. vanilla	4t	2T + 2t	¼c
1 t. grated lemon rind	2t	4t	2T
1 pint sour cream	1qt	2qt	3qt
3 T. sugar	6T	¾c	1c + 2T
Glaze			
½ cup sugar	1c	2c	3c
1 T. plus 1 t. cornstarch	2T + 2t	5T +1t	½c
½ cup water	1c	2c	3c
2 T. lemon juice	¼c	½c	¾c

Original recipe yields

12–16 servings

Cooking day instructions

Combine cracker crumbs, sugar, and butter. Press into bottom and sides of 12-inch springform pan. Bake at 350 degrees for 5 minutes. Cool.

Beat cream cheese at high speed until completely smooth. Add eggs, one at a time, beating until smooth after each egg. Continue to beat, gradually adding 1⅓ cups sugar, then lemon juice and 1 t. vanilla. Stir in lemon rind. Pour into cooled crust and bake at 350 degrees for 35 minutes.

▶

Blend sour cream with remaining 1 t. vanilla and 3 T. sugar. Set in warm place. Remove cake from oven. Gently spread sour cream mixture over top of cake. Return to oven and bake for 12 minutes. Cool on rack for 30 minutes. Refrigerate until topping is cool but not completely chilled.

Make glaze by combining sugar and cornstarch, then blending in water and lemon juice until smooth. Bring to a boil, stirring constantly, until thickened. Cook 3 minutes. Chill until cool but not set. Spread top of cheesecake with lemon glaze. Chill for 2 hours. Freeze by covering springform pan with plastic wrap and then sliding into a large freezer bag or completely wrapping in heavy-duty foil.

Serving day instructions

Thaw and serve.

Easy Pie Crust

The name says it all

	x3	x6	x9
1 cup flour	3c	6c	9c
1 t. salt	1T	2T	3T
⅓ cup shortening	1c	2c	3c
3 T. warm water	½c + 1T	1c + 2T	1½c + 3T

Original recipe yields

1 9- or 10-inch pie crust

Cooking day instructions

Mix flour and salt together with a fork. Cut shortening into flour mixture with a pastry cutter until well blended and evenly mixed. Blend in warm water with a fork, then work with hands until dough is smooth. Dough may be formed into disks and frozen at this point, using the freezer bag method, or may be assembled into pies (for example, Aunt Clara's Dutch Apple Pie) and frozen.

Serving day instructions

For whole pies, thaw or bake while still frozen, according to pie recipe directions. For pie dough disks, thaw and roll out to form pie crust.

English Toffee

You can't eat just one piece

1 cup sugar
1 cup unsalted butter
1 T. white corn syrup
Dash of salt
1 T. water
1¼ cups (6 oz.) almonds, chopped and toasted
10 oz. chocolate bar (milk or semisweet)

Original recipe yields

Approximately 5 dozen pieces

Cooking day instructions

We have had most success with making this recipe a single batch at a time and not trying to double or triple it.

Place sugar, butter, syrup, salt, and water in 2-quart saucepan. Quickly bring to a boil on high heat, stirring with wooden spoon. Stir constantly, cooking over medium-high heat until boiling mixture turns 1 shade darker than light brown sugar. Remove from heat and add 1 cup nuts. Pour into buttered 9x9 pan. Lay chocolate over and spread as chocolate melts to cover entire top. Sprinkle rest of nuts on top. Set at room temperature for one hour and refrigerate for 24 hours. Break into pieces and store in airtight container. Stores well in the refrigerator or freezer.

Freeze, using instructions for baked goods.

Frozen Chocolate Meringue Torte

Perfect for entertaining

	x2
4 large egg whites	8
¾ t. cream of tartar	1½t
1 cup sugar	2c
1 cup pecans, chopped	2c
2 cups whipping cream	4c
1 cup chocolate syrup	2c
1½ t. vanilla	1T
Chocolate shavings, for garnish	
Pecan halves, for garnish	

Serving day

Fresh strawberries or raspberries, for garnish

Original recipe yields

8–10 servings

Cooking day instructions

In large mixing bowl, beat egg whites until foamy. Add cream of tartar and beat until soft peaks form. Gradually add sugar, a little at a time, and continue beating until very soft peaks form. Fold in chopped pecans.

Cover 2 baking sheets with brown paper (or parchment paper). Draw an 8–10 inch diameter circle on each paper. Divide and spread meringue over each circle, shaping into flat shells. (See hint below.) Bake 45 minutes. Turn off oven. Do not remove meringues for another 45 minutes. *Do not open door.* Remove and cool. (Meringues may even be left in oven overnight.)

To assemble: In medium mixing bowl, beat cream until very stiff. Fold in chocolate syrup and vanilla. Spread meringue layer with half of chocolate cream. Add second meringue and cover top with remaining cream. Decorate with chocolate shavings and pecan halves. To serve that day, freeze at least 6 hours. To freeze for future use, use the foil and plastic wrap method.

Serving day instructions

Remove from freezer 20–30 minutes before serving. Garnish with fresh strawberries or raspberries.

Hint

For smaller, family-size portions, follow the same directions, except make 4 meringue shells, each measuring 5–6 inches across, yielding two tortes. Freeze one for later use.

Frozen Orange Dream Pie

A refreshing summer treat

	x2	x4	x6
6 oz. can frozen orange juice concentrate	12oz	24oz	36oz
1 pint vanilla ice cream, softened	1qt	2qt	3qt
1-11 oz. can mandarin oranges, drained and broken in pieces	2	4	6
4 cups whipped topping	8c	16c	24c
graham cracker crumb pie crust	2	4	6

Original recipe yields

1 pie

Cooking day instructions

In large bowl, beat orange juice concentrate for 30 seconds. Blend in ice cream. Fold in broken mandarin orange pieces and whipped topping. If necessary, freeze until mixture will mound.

Spoon mixture into graham cracker crust. Garnish with mandarin oranges and mint sprigs, if desired. Cover with plastic wrap, then foil. Freeze until firm, at least 4 hours.

Serving day instructions

Let stand at room temperature for 10 minutes before serving.

Frozen Pumpkin Dessert

A wonderful fall dessert

2 cups canned pumpkin
1 cup sugar
1 t. salt
1 t. ginger
1 t. cinnamon
½ t. nutmeg
1 cup chopped pecans
½ gallon vanilla ice cream, softened

Graham cracker crust

2 cups graham cracker crumbs
½ cup butter, melted
¼ cup sugar

Original recipe yields

24 servings

Cooking day instructions

Prepare graham cracker crust by mixing crust ingredients. Pat into 9x13 pan. Bake at 375 degrees for 10 minutes. Remove from oven and cool.

In large bowl, combine pumpkin, sugar, salt, spices, and nuts. Fold ice cream into pumpkin mixture. Pour pumpkin mixture into pan. Seal top of pan with plastic wrap, then foil. Freeze until firm.

Serving day instructions

Remove from freezer about 15 minutes before serving. Cut into squares and serve.

Heartland Brownies

Everybody loves brownies

	x2
1 cup butter, melted	2c
2 cups sugar	4c
½ cup baking cocoa	1c
4 eggs, beaten	8
2 t. vanilla	4t
1½ cups flour	3c
½ t. salt	1t
½ cup nuts (optional)	1c
Powdered sugar	

Original recipe yields

24 brownies (each 2 inches square)

Cooking day instructions

Combine butter, sugar, and baking cocoa. Add beaten eggs and vanilla. Mix together well. Beat in flour, salt, and nuts. Spread in greased 9x13 pan. Bake in a preheated 350-degree oven for 20–25 minutes. Test for doneness; do not overbake. Sprinkle powdered sugar over warm brownies. Cool brownies completely. Freeze, using instructions for baked goods.

Serving day instructions

Allow brownies to come to room temperature before serving.

Hint

Use these brownies as a base for decadent brownie sundaes. Top brownies with ice cream, Homemade Hot Fudge Sauce (see next page), nuts, and whipped cream.

Homemade Hot Fudge Sauce

Keep on hand for those nighttime ice cream cravings

1 cup sugar
4 T. butter (½ stick)
Dash of salt
1-5 oz. can evaporated milk
1½ squares unsweetened baking chocolate
1 t. vanilla extract
3 T. Grand Marnier (optional)

Original recipe yields

2 cups

Cooking day instructions

In saucepan over high heat, combine sugar, butter, salt, and milk. Bring to a boil, stirring constantly. Let sauce boil 3 minutes without stirring. Add chocolate and vanilla (and Grand Marnier, if desired). Stir until smooth. Serve at once over ice cream. Store 1 cup of sauce in refrigerator. Freeze other cup of sauce in a container that can be reheated in the microwave or in boiling water.

Serving day instructions

Allow sauce to thaw in refrigerator. Stir to mix, if needed. Reheat sauce in microwave or in a pan with boiling water, but do not allow to boil. Serve immediately.

Incredible Chocolate Fondue

Need we say more?

	x3	x6	x9
2 cups semisweet chocolate chips	6c	12c	18c
1/3 cup heavy cream	1c	2c	3c
1 T. sugar	3T	1/4c + 2T	1/2c + 1T
1/4 t. salt	3/4t	1 1/2t	2 1/4t
1/4 cup butter	3/4c	1 1/2c	2 1/4c
2 T. amaretto or vanilla extract	1/4c + 2T	3/4c	1c + 2T

Original recipe yields

2 1/2 cups fondue sauce

Cooking day instructions

In large saucepan, melt together chocolate chips, cream, sugar, and salt. Remove from heat and stir in butter and amaretto or vanilla. Cool. Freeze, using freezer bag method.

Serving day instructions

Allow sauce to thaw slightly. Place in fondue pot to heat, and serve with fresh fruit, pound cake, marshmallows, or anything you choose!

Light and Flaky Pie Crust

*Yes, you **can** make pie crust!*

	x3	x6	x9
1⅓ cups flour	4c	8c	12c
⅓ cup oil	1c	2c	3c
½ t. salt	1½t	1T	4½t
2 T. water	6T	¾c	1c + 2T

Original recipe yields

One pie crust (top or bottom)

Cooking day instructions

Place all ingredients in mixing bowl and mix together with fork until dough forms a ball. Roll out between two pieces of waxed paper. Remove top layer of waxed paper and place exposed side of crust in desired pie pan. Remove remaining layer of waxed paper. Shape or flute edge of pie crust to fit pan. Seal entire crust with plastic wrap so wrap is in direct contact with pie crust. Place in freezer bag or wrap with second layer of plastic wrap to freeze.

Serving day instructions

Preheat oven to 375 degrees. Bake 15–20 minutes or until golden brown, or fill according to desired recipe and follow instructions.

Hint

If preparing this pie crust at high altitude or in a dry climate, increase oil by 1–2 T. and water by 1–2 t. Dough should be moist and easy to work with.

Mom's Blueberry Pie

Berry, berry good!

	x3	x6	x9
4 cups blueberries	12c	24c	36c
2 heaping T. flour	¼c + 2T	¾c	1c + 2T
1 cup sugar	3c	6c	9c
1 T. butter	3T	6T	9T
¾ t. lemon juice	2¼t	4½t	2T + ¾t

Original recipe yields

One 9-inch pie

Cooking day instructions

Rinse berries in colander. Place berries in saucepan with flour, sugar, butter, and lemon juice, and bring just to boiling point. Pour in unbaked pie shell. Freeze, using foil and plastic wrap method.

Serving day instructions

Preheat oven to 375 degrees. Bake 40–50 minutes or until filling bubbles.

Hint

If pie crust is getting too brown before filling is done, cover lightly with foil and continue baking.

Oatmeal Chocolate Chip Cookies

The best we've found

	x2	x4
1 cup butter, softened	2c	4c
1 cup sugar	2c	4c
1 cup brown sugar	2c	4c
2 eggs	4	8
1 T. vanilla	2T	4T
2 cups flour	4c	8c
2½ cups oatmeal, powdered	5c	10c
½ t. salt	1t	2t
1 t. baking powder	2t	4t
1 t. baking soda	2t	4t
12 oz. chocolate chips	24oz	48oz
4 oz. Hershey chocolate bar, grated	8oz	16oz

Original recipe yields

4 dozen cookies

Cooking day instructions

Cream together butter and sugars. Add eggs and vanilla. Powder oatmeal by placing in a blender or food processor. Combine flour, powdered oatmeal, salt, baking powder, and baking soda. Add to butter and sugar mixture and mix well. Add in chocolate chips and grated Hershey bar. Form into golf ball–size balls. Bake at 350 degrees on ungreased cookie sheets for 9–11 minutes. Cool. Freeze, using instructions for baked goods.

Hints

For fresh-baked cookies, cookie dough balls may be flash frozen on cooking day, then thawed and baked on serving day.

Store baked cookies in freezer until serving day, as the oatmeal tends to go stale when cookies are left at room temperature for more than a day.

Peanut Butter Bars

Tastes just like a peanut butter cup

	x3
1 cup butter, melted	3c
1¾ cups graham cracker crumbs	5¼c
1 cup creamy peanut butter	3c
2⅓ cups powdered sugar	7c

Topping	
1 cup chocolate chips	3c
¾ cup peanut butter	2¼c

Original recipe yields

6 dozen bars

Cooking day instructions

Mix together butter, graham cracker crumbs, peanut butter, and sugar. Press into a buttered 9x13 pan.

For topping: Melt chocolate chips and peanut butter in saucepan and spread over bars. Cool and cut into squares. Freeze, using instructions for baked goods.

Serving day instructions

Thaw. Store in refrigerator until ready to serve.

Peanut Butter Monster Cookies

Kids go crazy for these

	x2
2 sticks margarine	4
2 cups brown sugar	4c
2 cups white sugar	4c
6 eggs	12
1½ t. Karo syrup	1T
2 T. baking soda	4T
1 T. vanilla	2T
3 cups peanut butter	6c
7½ cups rolled oats	15c
½ lb. chocolate chips	1 lb
½ lb. M&M's	1 lb

Original recipe yields

6½ dozen cookies

Cooking day instructions

Cream together margarine and sugars. Add eggs, Karo, soda, vanilla, and peanut butter. Beat well. Stir in oats, chocolate chips, and M&M's. Drop by teaspoonfuls onto ungreased cookie sheets and bake at 350 degrees for 10–12 minutes. Cool completely. Freeze, using instructions for baked goods. Note: there is no flour in this recipe!

Hint

For fresh-baked cookies, cookie dough balls may be flash frozen on cooking day, then thawed and baked on serving day.

Sugar Cookies

A cookie cutter basic

	x2	x4	x6
3 cups flour	6c	12c	18c
1 cup sugar	2c	4c	6c
½ t. salt	1t	2t	1T
1¼ cups shortening	2½c	5c	7½c
3 T. milk	6T	¾c	1c + 2T
1 t. cream of tartar	2t	4t	2T
2 eggs, beaten	4	8	12
1 t. vanilla	2t	4t	2T

Original recipe yields

5 dozen cookies

Cooking day instructions

Sift dry ingredients together. Cut in shortening. Add rest of ingredients. Roll out on countertop or cutting board, and cut with desired cookie cutters.

Bake at 400 degrees on ungreased cookie sheets for 7–10 minutes. Cool completely. Freeze, using instructions for baked goods.

Hints

Sprinkle with colored sugar prior to baking or frost with icing when cooled.

For fresh-baked cookies, cookie dough balls may be flash frozen on cooking day, then thawed and baked on serving day.

Brunch Items

Baked Blueberry French Toast
Breakfast Burritos
California Quiche
Christmas Quiche
Cream Cheese Apple Tart
Farmer's Casserole
Frozen Fruit Salad
Gooey Caramel Cinnamon Rolls
Mom's Breakfast Waffles
Western Slope Peach Cobbler

Baked Blueberry French Toast

A wonderful brunch affair

	x3	x6	x9
6 slices French bread, cubed	18	36	54
8 oz. package cream cheese, cubed	24oz	48oz	72oz
1-21 oz. can blueberry pie filling, divided	3	6	9
6 large eggs	18	36	54
¼ cup maple syrup	¾c	1½c	2¼c
1 cup milk	3c	6c	9c
½ t. cinnamon	1½t	1T	4½t

Original recipe yields

6–8 servings

Cooking day instructions

Butter an 8x8 baking dish. Place half the bread cubes in prepared dish. Scatter cream cheese cubes over first layer of bread cubes. Spoon half the can of pie filling in dollops over top and complete layering with remaining bread cubes. In medium mixing bowl, combine eggs, maple syrup, and milk. Whisk until well blended. Pour over existing layers. Spread remaining blueberry pie filling over top, then sprinkle with cinnamon. Freeze, using foil and plastic wrap method.

Serving day instructions

Thaw completely. Preheat oven to 350 degrees. Cover baking dish with foil and bake covered for 30 minutes. Remove foil from dish and continue baking uncovered for an additional 30 minutes. Place in individual serving bowls and serve warm with maple syrup.

Substitution

Other fruit pie fillings may be substituted.

Breakfast Burritos

A hearty meal for breakfast on the run

	x3	x6	x9
½ lb. ground pork sausage	1½ lbs	3 lbs	4½ lbs
½ lb. frozen cubed Ore Ida potatoes	1½ lbs	3 lbs	4½ lbs
6 eggs, beaten	18	36	54
1 T. milk	3T	¼c + 2T	½c + 1T
½ t. salt	1½t	1T	4½t
¼ t. pepper	¾t	1½t	2¼t
1 T. butter	3T	6T	9T
1-10 oz. can green chili sauce	3	6	9
6–8 burrito-size flour tortillas	18–24	36–48	54–72
1 cup cheddar cheese	3c	6c	9c

Original recipe yields

6–8 servings

Cooking day instructions

In large skillet, brown sausage. Remove from heat and drain excess fat. Set aside. Brown potatoes in oven by placing on cookie sheet and broiling according to package directions until crisp. Meanwhile, mix eggs, milk, salt, and pepper together in medium mixing bowl. Over medium heat, melt butter in separate large skillet. Add egg mixture to skillet and scramble eggs, removing from heat once eggs are cooked but still moist. Warm green chili over medium heat in saucepan until heated through.

To assemble burritos: Warm flour tortillas on skillet or griddle until flexible, turning once. Fill tortillas with ⅓ cup scrambled eggs, 2–3 T. sausage, and ⅓ cup potatoes. Top with cheddar cheese and green chili according to taste. Fold filled tortillas into burritos. Wrap each burrito in plastic wrap, then place individual burritos in freezer bags. Freeze.

Serving day instructions

Remove individual burritos from freezer. Place frozen burrito in microwave, and heat on high setting for 2–3 minutes or until heated through. If additional heating is needed, warm on high by 30-second increments.

Substitutions

Red salsa may be substituted for green chili. Turkey sausage may be substituted.

California Quiche

A quiche with a southwestern flair

	x3	x6	x9
3 eggs	9	18	27
1 cup milk	3c	6c	9c
¼ t. salt	¾t	1½t	2¼t
1½ cups grated Monterey Jack cheese	4½c	9c	13½c
9-inch pie crust	3	6	9
1 small can diced green chiles	3	6	9
1 cup grated cheddar cheese	3c	6c	9c

Original recipe yields

4 large servings

Cooking day instructions

Beat eggs with milk and salt. Spread Monterey Jack cheese over bottom of pie crust. Spread green chiles over cheese, then pour egg mixture over chiles. Place cheddar on top, and bake in disposable aluminum pie pans in a 400-degree oven for 40 minutes or just until knife inserted in center comes out clean. Freeze, leaving quiche in pie pan, using freezer bag method.

Serving day instructions

Thaw quiche thoroughly and place in warm oven just until heated through.

Christmas Quiche

Wonderful any time of the year!

	x2	x4	x6
3 cups shredded Swiss cheese	6c	12c	18c
12 strips bacon, cooked and crumbled	24	48	72
½ cup mushrooms, finely chopped	1c	2c	3c
3 T. green onions, sliced	6T	¾c	1c + 2T
5 eggs, slightly beaten	10	20	30
2¼ cups light cream or half and half	4½c	9c	13½c
Salt and pepper to taste			
Dash of nutmeg			
2 T. grated Parmesan cheese (fresh is best)	¼c	½c	¾c
2 9-inch unbaked pastry shells	4	8	12

Original recipe yields

Two (9-inch) quiches

Cooking day instructions

Combine all ingredients but the last together, and place in unbaked pastry shell. Bake at 375 degrees for 30–35 minutes, just until a knife inserted in center comes out clean.

Serving day instructions

Thaw completely. To reheat, bake quiche at 350–375 degrees for approximately 20–30 minutes or until heated through.

Hints

If freezing, slightly underbake so quiche is not overcooked when heated again in the oven.

To avoid overbrowning the crust or top during reheating, use foil around pie crust edges.

Cream Cheese Apple Tart

Also great for dessert

	x2	x4
Crust (See hint below)		
1¼ cups flour	2½c	5c
⅓ cup sugar	⅔c	1⅓c
¼ t. nutmeg	½t	1t
½ t. baking powder	1t	2t
½ t. salt	1t	2t
½ cup (1 stick) unsalted butter, chilled	1c	2c
1 egg	2	4
1 T. milk	2T	¼c
Filling		
8 oz. package cream cheese, softened	16oz	32oz
¼ cup sugar	½c	1c
2 egg yolks	4	8
½ t. vanilla extract	1t	2t
Topping		
2 large McIntosh apples, peeled, cored, and thinly sliced	4	8
⅓ cup sugar	⅔c	1⅓c
½ t. cornstarch	1t	2t
½ t. ground cinnamon	1t	2t

Original recipe yields

6–8 servings

Cooking day instructions

In large bowl or food processor, combine flour, ⅓ cup sugar, nutmeg, baking powder, and salt. Cut butter into flour mixture until crumbly. In small bowl, beat egg and milk and add to flour mixture. Blend until dough forms a ball. Pat dough into disposable pie pan.

With electric mixer or food processor, blend cream cheese and ¼ cup sugar. With mixer running, add egg yolks and vanilla and blend until smooth. Spread evenly over crust. Layer apples over cream cheese mixture, in circular pattern, slightly overlapping slices. In small bowl, combine remaining ⅓ cup sugar, cornstarch, and cinnamon and sprinkle over apples. Cover pie plate tightly with plastic wrap and then foil. Label.

Serving day instructions

Thaw. Bake 30 minutes at 350 degrees. Reduce oven temperature to 300 degrees and continue baking 10 more minutes or until golden brown.

Hint

Crust is better if made in smaller batches. It can be doubled with good results, but if making x4, make 2 batches of dough and divide filling and topping. If you overwork dough, it becomes tough.

Farmer's Casserole

Great for lunch or dinner!

	x3	x6	x9
3 cups frozen shredded hash brown potatoes (24 oz. bag)	9c	18c	27c
¾ cup shredded Monterey Jack cheese (3–4 oz.)	2¼c	4½c	6¾c
¾ cup shredded cheddar cheese (3–4 oz.)	2¼c	4½c	6¾c
1 cup diced ham or Canadian-style bacon (5 oz.)	3c	6c	9c
1-4.5 oz. can mild green chiles (optional)	3	6	9
¼ cup green onions, sliced (2–3 medium)	¾c	1½c	2¼c
4 beaten eggs (or 1 cup frozen egg product)	12	24	36
1-12 oz. can evaporated milk	3	6	9
¼ t. pepper	¾t	1½t	2¼t
⅛ t. salt	⅜t	¾t	1⅛t

Original recipe yields

6 servings

Cooking day instructions

Grease a 2-quart square baking dish. Arrange potatoes evenly in bottom of dish. Sprinkle with cheeses, ham, green chiles, and green onions. In medium mixing bowl, combine eggs, milk, pepper, and salt. Pour egg mixture over potato mixture in dish. (If not freezing, cover and chill several hours or overnight, then follow serving day suggestions.) Freeze, using the plastic wrap and foil method.

Serving day instructions

Thaw completely. Bake uncovered in a 350-degree oven for 40–45 minutes or until center appears set. Let stand 5 minutes before serving. If you prefer, extra shredded cheese can be sprinkled on top during the last 15 minutes of baking.

Frozen Fruit Salad

An easy, beautiful side dish for entertaining

	x2	x4
1-8 oz. pkg. cream cheese, room temperature	2 pkgs	4 pkgs
2 T. mayonnaise	¼c	½c
1-15.5 oz. can fruit cocktail, drained (see below)	2	4
1 small can crushed pineapple, drained	2	4
½ pint whipped cream	1pt	1qt
2 T. sugar	¼c	½c
1 cup pecans or almonds, chopped (optional)	2c	3–4c
Maraschino cherries to decorate, halved, drained, and blotted on paper towel		

Original recipe yields

12–15 servings (approximately 2½ x 2½ square)

Cooking day instructions

Blend cream cheese and mayonnaise together. Mix fruit cocktail (or canned fruit of choice) and drained pineapple with cream cheese mixture. Whip the cream with sugar. Gently fold the cream cheese mixture along with ¾ cup nuts (optional) into the whipped cream, mixing thoroughly. Spread evenly into 9x13 pan. Sprinkle remaining ¼ cup chopped nuts on top. Place maraschino cherries 1½ inch apart so that each piece, when cut, will have a cherry in the middle. Cover with plastic wrap so that wrap touches surface of fruit salad. Then cover with heavy foil and freeze.

Serving day instructions

Take out of freezer 15–20 minutes before serving. Using a warm knife (dipped in warm water), score and cut frozen salad into even squares, so that a cherry is centered in each piece. Garnish with mint or decorative lettuce leaves.

Hints

Using canned Queen Anne cherries, this makes a festive side salad for Christmas, or for any special occasion.

To use as a side dish for any meal, consider freezing meal-size quantities (4–6 squares) in smaller square or oblong containers. Then pop them out at a moment's notice!

Substitutions

Instead of fruit cocktail, you can use any of the following canned fruit: blueberries, Queen Anne cherries, mandarin oranges, or a combination.

Kids love this salad when miniature marshmallows (⅔ package, about 2 cups) are added along with the fruit.

Gooey Caramel Cinnamon Rolls

Serve these while still warm

	x2	x3
Dough (see hint)		
3½ cups flour	7c	10½c
1 package active dry yeast	2 pkgs	3 pkgs
1¼ cups milk	2½c	3¾c
¼ cup sugar	½c	¾c
¼ cup shortening	½c	¾c
1 t. salt	2t	1T
1 egg	2	3
Filling		
½ cup melted butter	1c	1½c
½ cup brown sugar or sugar	1c	1½c
2 t. ground cinnamon	4t	2T
Caramel topping		
1 cup brown sugar	2c	3c
½ cup butter	1c	1½c
2 T. light corn syrup	¼c	¼c + 2T
½ cup or more chopped pecans (optional)	1c	1½c

Original recipe yields

2–2½ dozen rolls (depending on thickness); two 8x8 or 9x9 pans

Cooking day instructions

In mixing bowl, combine 1½ cups flour and the yeast. In a medium saucepan, heat milk, sugar, shortening, and salt just until warm (115–120 degrees), stirring constantly until shortening almost melts. Add to dry mixture; add egg. Beat at low speed with electric mixer for 30 seconds, scraping bowl. Beat 3 minutes at high speed. By hand or with mixer on low speed, stir in remaining flour to make a soft dough. Shape into a ball. Place in a lightly greased bowl, turning once to grease surface. Cover and let rise in warm place until dough doubles in size (approximately 1½–2 hours).

Meanwhile, blend filling ingredients together in a bowl. Set aside.

Prepare caramel topping: In a medium saucepan, mix the brown sugar, butter, and corn syrup. Heat slowly, stirring often. Add pecans, if desired.

When dough has risen, punch down and turn onto a floured surface. Cover and let rest for 10 minutes. Divide dough in half and roll out one piece into a 16x8 rectangle. Spread half of filling mixture over entire surface. Roll up jelly-roll style, starting with long edge; seal edges by pinching together. Cut in 1½-inch slices. Repeat with other half of dough.

Line two baking pans (using the plastic wrap and foil method) or use disposable aluminum baking pans, and divide caramel topping into each pan. Place rolls, cut side down, over mixture. Seal well, label, and freeze. If serving rolls that day, let rise in warm place until doubled in size, 30–45 minutes.

Serving day instructions

Be sure to remove outer wrap from cinnamon rolls while still frozen and return frozen rolls to pans with the caramel mixture facing down. Thaw and let rise in warm place until doubled in size. Bake at 375 degrees about 20 minutes. Cool 2–3 minutes, then invert onto a plate or tray and remove pan.

Hint

This recipe is better if the dough is prepared in single batches, rather than doubling or tripling, as the dough will get too tough if mixed in large quantities. The filling and topping ingredients can be doubled or tripled and then divided.

Mom's Breakfast Waffles

Serve with fresh fruit for breakfast in bed

	x2	x4
3 cups flour	6c	12c
5 t. baking powder	3T + 1t	6T + 2t
1 t. salt	2t	4t
1 T. sugar	2T	4T
4 large eggs	8	16
2¼ cups milk	4½c	9c
1½ t. vanilla	1T	2T
⅔ cup vegetable oil or butter, melted	1⅓c	2⅔c

Original recipe yields

14–18 waffles (approximately 5 inches square)

Cooking day instructions

Measure flour, baking powder, salt, and sugar into large mixing bowl. In separate bowl, beat eggs on high speed for 1 minute. Add milk and vanilla to eggs. Add this mixture to dry ingredients. Beat on medium speed about 1½ minutes until well blended. Slowly add oil or butter and beat on low speed until blended.

Heat waffle iron and brush lightly with cooking oil or spray. Pour about ½–¾ cup waffle mixture in middle of each waffle grid (depending on size of your waffle iron). Gently spread mixture evenly over grid. Bake according to your waffle iron instructions. Consider slightly underbaking waffles, so that they are done but not completely browned. This will keep waffles moist when reheated in toaster or microwave. Freeze breakfast-size portions, using instructions for baked goods.

Serving day instructions

Thaw completely. For a crispy texture, pop waffles in toaster or toaster oven. The oven can also be used to heat several at one time. Place on cookie sheet in a preheated 375–400-degree oven for 10–15 minutes or until heated through. Serve with butter, warm syrup, powdered sugar, or fresh or frozen fruit on top.

Hint

Toasted pecans or almonds make a nice addition to this batter. Sprinkle them on top of waffle batter just before cooking waffles.

Substitution

This batter can be used for pancakes as well. Adjust the milk ratio, depending on the type of pancakes you like—thick (use less milk) or thin (use more milk).

Western Slope Peach Cobbler

Serve warm with ice cream

	x3	x6	x9
Filling			
1½ cups sugar	4½c	9c	13½c
⅓ cup cornstarch	1c	2c	3c
½ t. cinnamon	1½t	1T	4½t
¼ t. almond extract	¾t	1½t	2¼t
6–8 fresh peaches, peeled and sliced, enough to fill a 9x13 baking dish	18–24	36–48	54–72
Topping (serving day)			
1 cup sugar			
1 cup flour			
1 t. baking powder			
1 large egg			
1 stick margarine			

Original recipe yields

18–24 servings

Cooking day instructions

Mix 1½ cups sugar, cornstarch, cinnamon, and almond extract. Add fresh fruit to mixture, place in freezer bag, and freeze, using freezer bag method.

Serving day instructions

Thaw fruit filling. Pour into greased 9x13 baking dish. For topping, mix sugar, flour, and baking powder. Beat egg and mix with flour/sugar mixture until crumbly. Sprinkle over fruit. Melt margarine and drizzle over top. Bake at 350 degrees for 45–60 minutes, until light brown.

Hint

For an easy way to peel peaches, plunge them in boiling water for 1–2 minutes, then in cold water. The peels will slide right off!

Substitution

Other fresh fruit, such as cherries, apples, or berries, may be substituted for the peaches. The amount of sugar in the filling may need to be adjusted, depending on the tartness of the fruit.

Add a Side Dish

Bacon-Cheese New Potatoes
Baked Broccoli Medley
Broccoli Casserole
Cheese Vegetables
Corn Casserole
Festive Corn and Broccoli
Hash Brown Casserole
Parmesan Green Beans
Potatoes Divine
Rice Broccoli Casserole

Bacon-Cheese New Potatoes

Makes a tasty side dish for company or a dinner party!

	x3	x6	x9
1½ lbs. unpeeled new potatoes	4½ lbs	9 lbs	13½ lbs
2 T. olive oil	6T	¾c	1c + 2T
1 cup (2 oz.) finely shredded Gruyère cheese	3c	6c	9c
½ cup sour cream	1½c	3c	4½c
½ cup green onions, minced	1½c	3c	4½c
1-3 oz. package cream cheese, softened	3	6	9
2 T. minced fresh basil or 1 t. dried basil leaves	6T (1T)	¾c (2T)	1c + 2T (3T)
1 clove garlic, minced	3	6	9
¼ t. salt	¾t	1½t	2¼t
¼ t. ground black pepper	¾t	1½t	2¼t
8 oz. bacon, cooked and finely chopped	24oz	48oz	72oz

Original recipe yields

About 26 potato halves

Cooking day instructions

Preheat oven to 400 degrees. Rub potatoes with olive oil and place on ungreased baking sheet; bake 1 hour or until tender. Allow potatoes to cool enough to handle. Cut potatoes in half. Cut a small slice off bottom of each potato half so potato will sit flat. Using a small melon baller, scoop out a small portion of potato pulp, leaving at least a ¼-inch shell; reserve potato pulp.

In bowl, combine potato pulp and next 8 ingredients with an electric mixer; stir in bacon. Spoon potato mixture into each potato shell. Wrap plastic wrap thoroughly around each potato, then place in freezer bag. Freeze, using freezer bag method.

Serving day instructions

Thaw completely. Place potatoes on greased baking sheet. In a preheated 350-degree oven, bake 15–20 minutes or until lightly browned. Serve warm.

Baked Broccoli Medley

A healthy vegetable bake

1 large bunch broccoli, trimmed, or 2-10 oz. packages frozen broccoli, thawed

4 tomatoes, quartered

2 onions, sliced

2 green peppers, sliced

1 cup mushrooms, sliced

2 packages (10 oz.) Cracker Barrel cheddar cheese, sliced

1 t. sugar

1 t. garlic salt

½ t. pepper

Original recipe yields

12 servings

Serving day instructions

This vegetable dish is best when made on the day it is to be served. Grease a 9x13 baking dish. Combine broccoli, tomatoes, onions, green peppers, and mushrooms. Layer half of vegetables in baking dish and top with half of cheese. Combine seasonings and sprinkle half on cheese layer. Add remaining vegetables and sprinkle with remaining seasonings and cheese. Bake at 350 degrees for 30 minutes covered, then 45 minutes uncovered.

Broccoli Casserole

Nice for holiday entertaining

	x2
1½ bunches broccoli, cooked	3
1 can undiluted cream of mushroom soup	2
½ cup sour cream	1c
1 T. lemon juice	2T
½ cup grated sharp cheddar cheese	1c
1-4 oz. jar pimientos	8oz
1 cup crushed cheese crackers	2c
¼ cup broken almonds	½c
¼ cup water chestnuts, diced (optional)	½c

Original recipe yields

6–8 servings

Serving day instructions

This casserole is best when made on the day it is to be served. Place broccoli in baking dish. Mix together soup, sour cream, lemon juice, and cheese, and spoon over broccoli. Sprinkle pimientos on top and top with crackers, nuts, and water chestnuts. Bake uncovered at 350 degrees for 25 minutes.

Cheese Vegetables

Your kids will eat this!

1-24 oz. bag frozen California blend vegetables

1 stick margarine, melted

10 oz. Velveeta cheese, melted

30 Ritz crackers, crushed

Original recipe yields

6 servings

Serving day instructions

This dish is best when made on the day it is to be served. Cook vegetables according to package directions. Drain. Mix half of margarine with cheese and half with crushed crackers. Add cheese mixture to vegetables. Place cheese and vegetable mixture in 1½-quart baking dish. Top with crushed cracker mixture. Bake uncovered at 350 degrees for 20 minutes or until bubbly.

Corn Casserole

Great complement to your turkey dinner

1 stick margarine
1 can creamed corn
1 can whole kernel corn
2 t. sugar
3 eggs, beaten
1 cup sour cream
1 package Jiffy corn muffin mix
1-8 oz. package mozzarella cheese

Original recipe yields

6–8 servings

Serving day instructions

This dish is best when made on the day it is to be served. Melt margarine in 2-quart casserole dish. Stir in all ingredients except half the package of mozzarella cheese. Bake at 350 degrees for 45–60 minutes. During the last 15 minutes, add rest of cheese over top. Bake until cheese is melted.

Festive Corn and Broccoli

A simple, pretty dish

	x2
½ cup butter	1c
1-12 oz. can Mexicorn	24oz
1-10 oz. pkg. frozen broccoli, or 1 fresh bunch	20oz (2 bunches)
1 t. basil	2t
½ t. salt	1t
⅛ t. garlic powder	¼t
⅛ t. pepper	¼t

Original recipe yields

6 servings

Serving day instructions

This dish is best when made on the day it is to be served. Melt butter in saucepan; add remaining ingredients. Cover and cook for 8–10 minutes, until vegetables are tender but still crisp.

Hash Brown Casserole

A summertime side with burgers and brats

	x2	x4
2 lb. bag frozen hash browns	4 lb	8 lb
1 pint sour cream	2pts	4pts
2 cans cream of chicken soup	4	8
⅓ cup chopped onion	⅔c	1⅓c

Serving day

12 oz. grated cheddar cheese

Original recipe yields

8–10 servings

Cooking day instructions

Mix together hash browns, sour cream, soup, and onion, and place in lined 9x13 dish. Freeze, using the foil and plastic wrap method.

Serving day instructions

Thaw completely. Bake at 350 degrees for 1½ hours. Top with cheese during the last half hour.

Parmesan Green Beans

Give it a try—you'll love it

2-10 oz. packages frozen French-cut green beans
3 T. butter
2 T. flour
1½ cups sour cream
1 t. salt
1 t. grated lemon rind
¼ t. pepper
½ cup onion, diced
1 T. parsley, minced
½ cup fresh grated Parmesan cheese

Original recipe yields

4–6 servings

Serving day instructions

This dish is best when made on the day it is to be served. Prepare green beans according to package directions. Drain well. In large bowl, combine all ingredients and pour into 1½-quart baking dish. Bake at 325 degrees for 30 minutes.

Potatoes Divine

A touch of heaven on earth!

	x3	x6	x9
3 lbs. russet potatoes, pricked with fork	9 lbs	18 lbs	27 lbs
¼ cup butter, softened	¾c	1½c	2¼c
½ cup milk	1½c	3c	4½c

Serving day

¾ cup whipping cream

3 oz. Gruyère cheese, grated

3 T. freshly grated Parmesan cheese

Chopped fresh parsley

Original recipe yields

6–8 servings

Cooking day instructions

Preheat oven to 400 degrees. Place potatoes directly on oven rack and bake 45–60 minutes or until easily pierced with fork. Remove from oven, cool slightly, and halve lengthwise. Grease 13x9x2 or 3-quart baking pan. Scrape out potato flesh. Mash potato flesh with electric mixer or hand masher until smooth. Add butter and milk and stir until blended. Spread in prepared pan. Freeze, using foil and plastic wrap method.

Serving day instructions

When potatoes are thawed, preheat oven to 500 degrees. With electric mixer, whip cream to soft peaks, then fold in Gruyère by hand. Spread evenly over potatoes and sprinkle with Parmesan. Bake until heated thoroughly and topping is golden brown. Garnish with parsley and serve warm.

Rice Broccoli Casserole

Serve with your favorite chicken dish

1 small onion, chopped
½ cup margarine
1-10 oz. pkg. frozen broccoli, chopped
1 can cream of mushroom soup
8 oz. Velveeta cheese
1 cup cooked rice

Original recipe yields

8–10 servings

Serving day instructions

This dish is best when made on the day it is to be served. Brown onion in margarine. Add broccoli and stir until thawed. Add soup, then cheese, and stir until melted. Add rice to soup mixture and place in 2-quart baking dish. Bake at 350 degrees for 20–30 minutes.

Equivalency Chart

Ounces	Tablespoon	Teaspoon	Cups
-	1	3	-
1	2	6	-
2	4	12	1/4
-	5 1/3	-	1/3
3	6	18	-
4	8	24	1/2
5	10	30	-
-	10 2/3	-	2/3
6	12	36	3/4
7	14	42	-
8	16	48	1

2 cups	1 pint
4 cups	1 quart
4 quarts	1 gallon
16 oz.	1 pound
32 oz.	1 quart
1 medium lemon	3 T. juice
1 medium orange	1/3 cup juice
1 medium onion, chopped	1/2 cup
2 cups granulated sugar	1 pound
3 1/2 cups powdered sugar	1 pound
2 1/2 cups brown sugar	1 pound
7 oz. spaghetti	4 cups cooked
4 oz. uncooked noodles (1 1/2–2 cups)	2–3 cups cooked
1 cup uncooked long grain rice	3–4 cups cooked
1 stick butter or margarine	1/2 cup
1 cup nuts, chopped	1/4 pound
4 cups grated cheese	1 pound
Grated peel of lemon	1 T.
Grated peel of orange	2 T.
1 cup whipping cream	2 cups whipped

Bibliography

Fraser, Linda. *Best Ever Chicken*. London: Hermes House, 2003.

Junior League of Albuquerque. *Simply Simpatico*. Albuquerque: Junior League of Albuquerque, 1987.

Junior League of Denver. *Colorado Cache*. Denver: Junior League of Denver, 1978.

———. *Colorado Collage*. Denver: Junior League of Denver, 1995.

———. *Colorado Colore*. Denver: Junior League of Denver, 2002.

———. *Creme de Colorado Cookbook*. Denver: Junior League of Denver, 1987.

Junior League of Indianapolis. *Winners*. Indianapolis: Junior League of Indianapolis, 1985.

Junior League of Portland. *From Portland's Palate*. Portland: Junior League of Portland, 1987.

Kappa, Kappa, Kappa of South Bend. *Bill of Fare*. New York: Dover Publications, 1985.

Leisure Arts. *The Spirit of Christmas, Book 6*. Little Rock: Leisure Arts, Inc., 1992.

McKee, Gwen, and Barbara Mosely. *Best of the Best from Colorado*. Brandon, MO: Quail Ridge Press, 1998.

Purviance, Jamie, and Sandra S. McRae. *Weber's Big Book of Grilling*. San Francisco: Chronicle Books, 2001.

Stoltzfus, Louise. *Favorite Recipes From Quilters*. Intercourse, Pennsylvania: Good Books, 1992.

Wright, Jeni. *The Cook's Encyclopedia of Pasta*. New York: Anness Publishing, 2002.

Index of Recipes

Appetizers and Beverages

Apricot-Glazed Chicken Tenders, 30
Apricot Nectar Slush, 32
Caribbean Cooler, 33
Elegant Mushroom Cups, 34
Gourmet Palmiers, 35
Holiday Fruit Punch, 37
Kansas City Hot Wings, 38
Orange Beef Lettuce Wraps, 39
Refreshing Fruit Smoothies, 41
Santa Fe Hot Dip, 42
South of the Border Queso, 43
Strawberry Freeze, 44

Beef and Pork

Baked Steak in Tangy Tomato Sauce, 118
Barbecue Spareribs, 119
Beef Chimichangas, 120
Beef Fajitas, 122
Beef Kabobs Dijon, 124
Beef Pita Tacos, 125
Beef Stroganoff, 126
Colorado Style Beef Enchiladas, 127
Continental Beef, 129
Cottage Pie, 131
Dijon Pork Loin Roast, 132
French Steak, 133
Honey Pork Chops, 135
Lemony Flank Steak, 136
London Broil, 137
Meatballs, 139
Molasses-Bourbon Short Ribs, 141
Pinwheel Flank Steak, 143
Pork Chops à la Orange, 145
Rio Rancho Taco Meat, 146
Rocky Mountain Beef Brisket with Barbecue Sauce, 147
Sassy Sloppy Joes, 149
Shish-Ka-Bobs, 150
Shredded Salsa Beef, 151
Sirloin Strips in Wine Sauce, 152
Steak/Chicken Picado, 153
Venezuelan Steak, 154
Very Best Meatloaf, 156
Woodland Park Italian Beef, 158

Breads and Muffins

Chocolate-Orange Crumb Cake, 46
Classic Crumb Cake, 48
Easy No-Knead Rolls, 50
Honey Whole Wheat Bread, 51
Lemon Bread, 52
Orange Sour Cream Loaf, 53
Poppy Seed Pound Cake Muffins, 54
Pumpkin Chocolate Chip Loaf, 55
Quick and Delicious Banana Bread, 56
Sour Cream Muffins, 57
True Blue Muffins, 59
White River Sour Cream Cornbread, 60

Brunch Items

Baked Blueberry French Toast, 204
Breakfast Burritos, 205
California Quiche, 207
Christmas Quiche, 208
Cream Cheese Apple Tart, 209
Farmer's Casserole, 211
Frozen Fruit Salad, 212
Gooey Caramel Cinnamon Rolls, 214
Mom's Breakfast Waffles, 216
Western Slope Peach Cobbler, 218

Desserts

Almond Cookies, 178
Aunt Clara's Dutch Apple Pie, 179
Cashew Fudge Tarts, 180
Chocolate Butter Cookies, 181
Chocolate Mint Snaps, 182
Chocolate Orange Mousse, 183
Coconut Buttons, 184
Creamy Lemon Cheesecake, 185
Easy Pie Crust, 187
English Toffee, 188
Frozen Chocolate Meringue Torte, 189
Frozen Orange Dream Pie, 191
Frozen Pumpkin Dessert, 192
Heartland Brownies, 193
Homemade Hot Fudge Sauce, 194
Incredible Chocolate Fondue, 195
Light and Flaky Pie Crust, 196
Mom's Blueberry Pie, 197
Oatmeal Chocolate Chip Cookies, 198
Peanut Butter Bars, 199
Peanut Butter Monster Cookies, 200
Sugar Cookies, 201

Pasta and More

Barbecue Chicken Pizza, 160
Chicken Alfredo Pizza, 161
Italian Sausage and Green Pepper
  Cannoli, 162
Manicotti, 164
No-Fail Egg Noodles, 165
No-Rise Pizza Dough, 167
Penne with Chicken, Broccoli, and
  Cheese, 169
Quick Mix Pizza Dough, 170
Spaghetti Carbonara, 171
Spaghetti Sauce, 172
Spinach Lasagna, 174

Poultry

Buttermilk Herb Chicken Breasts, 80
Cheesy Chicken Bundles, 81
Chicken à la King, 82
Chicken Breasts in Phyllo, 83
Chicken Breasts Stuffed with Pesto
  Butter, 84
Chicken Cacciatore, 86
Chicken Cilantro Enchiladas, 87
Chicken Enchiladas, 89
Chicken Lelani, 90
Chicken Parisienne, 91
Chicken Pot Pie, 92
Chicken in Raspberry Sauce, 94
Chicken Wellington, 95
Cranberry Chicken, 97
Elegant Chicken Roll, 98
Grilled Turkey Breast with Peanut
  Sauce, 99
Hawaiian Chicken, 101
Honey Pecan Chicken, 102
Italian Stuffed Chicken Breasts, 104
Lemon Glazed Chicken Breasts, 106
Orange Teriyaki Chicken, 107
Oriental Sesame Chicken Strips, 108
Pecan Stuffed Chicken Breasts, 109
Polynesian Chicken Bundles, 111
Teriyaki Chicken (or Steak), 112

Tropical Chicken Ribbons, 113
Turkey Picante Pie, 114

Side Dishes

Bacon-Cheese New Potatoes, 222
Baked Broccoli Medley, 223
Broccoli Casserole, 224
Cheese Vegetables, 225
Corn Casserole, 226
Festive Corn and Broccoli, 227
Hash Brown Casserole, 228
Parmesan Green Beans, 229
Potatoes Divine, 230
Rice Broccoli Casserole, 231

Soup

Broccoli Cheese Soup, 62
Chicken Noodle Soup, 63
Chicken Tortilla Soup, 64
Chili (New Mexico style), 66
Chili Con Carne, 68
Colorado White Chili, 69
Cream of Split Pea Soup, 71
French Onion Soup, 72
North Woods Wild Rice Soup, 73
Old-Time Beef Stew, 74
Taco Soup, 75
Tomato and Leek Bisque, 76

Susie Martinez is a mother of two who works as a counselor and is a graduate student at Colorado Christian University. She graduated from Taylor University with a major in social work. Susie enjoys home decorating and is licensed to teach family and consumer studies. An Indiana native, Susie has been married to her husband, Joe, for eighteen years.

Vanda Howell is a busy mom who works part-time as a kitchen design consultant while raising her son. She attended Colorado State University, majoring in business and art. Vanda enjoys gourmet cooking and gardening. She sings on the worship team and is the administrator for the performing arts ministry of her local church. Vanda, a Denver native, has been married to her husband, Mike, for twenty-three years.

Bonnie Garcia is a busy mother of three sons who works part-time as a pediatric nurse. She graduated from Grace College with a degree in nursing. In addition to cooking, she also enjoys creating photo scrapbooks. An Iowa native, Bonnie has been married to her husband, Steve, for twenty-two years. She is active in her local church, where her husband is the senior pastor.

If you'd like more information about our fun and informative seminars in your area, contact us for a fee schedule and availability.

Don't Panic . . . Dinner's in the Freezer!
Phone: 303-980-9850
Fax: 303-980-9852
Email: udontpanic@aol.com